FEARLESS FAITH

Standing Firm in Freedom and Hope

A Study of Galatians, 1 & 2 Thessalonians

Jack W. Hayford, Jr.
with
Jack W. Hayford, III

THOMAS NELSON PUBLISHERS
Nashville • Atlanta • London • Vancouver

CONTENTS
. . . .

Fearless Faith: Standing Firm in Freedom and Hope (*A Study of Galatians, 1 & 2 Thessalonians*) is one of a series of study guides that focus exciting, discovery-geared coverage of Bible book and power themes—all prompting toward dynamic, Holy Spirit-filled living.

About the Executive Editor

JACK W. HAYFORD, noted pastor, teacher, writer, and composer, is the Executive Editor of the complete series, working with the publisher in conceiving and developing each of the books.

Dr. Hayford is Senior Pastor of The Church On The Way, the First Foursquare Church of Van Nuys, California. He and his wife, Anna, have four married children, all of whom are active in either pastoral ministry or vital church life. As General Editor of the *Spirit-Filled Life Bible*, Pastor Hayford led a four-year project, which has resulted in the availability of one of today's most practical and popular study Bibles. He is author of more than twenty books, including *A Passion for Fullness, The Beauty of Spiritual Language, Rebuilding the Real You*, and *Prayer Is Invading the Impossible*. His musical compositions number over four hundred songs, including the widely sung "Majesty."

About the Writer

JACK HAYFORD III is a scientific technician who has worked as a paper chemist. He is a chemistry graduate (with honors) from Azusa Pacific University in California and did his graduate work at Lawrence University in Appleton, Wisconsin, at the Institute of Paper Science and Technology. He is a member and actively involved in teaching in his local congregation, where he and his wife, Joann serve. They have two children: Dawn and Jack IV.

Jack's teacher/scientist bent early manifested itself when, as a pastor's son, he taught himself New Testament Greek as a side hobby, along with his interest in chess and wrestling as a member of the Los Angeles High School Championship Team.

His deep interest in Bible and theology made him an able assistant to his father during the editorial preparation of the *Spirit-Filled Life Bible*, released by Thomas Nelson Publishers in 1991.

Of this contributor, the Executive Editor has remarked: "It's a privilege to be involved with Jack in exacting areas of Christian life and thought. His thoroughness of thinking gives his work a quality that will profit every student."

THE GIFT
THAT KEEPS ON GIVING

One of the most precious gifts God has given us is His Word, the Bible. Wrapped in the glory and sacrifice of His Son and delivered by the power and ministry of His Spirit, it is a treasured gift—the gift that keeps on giving, because the Giver it reveals is inexhaustible in His love and grace.

Tragically, though, fewer and fewer people are opening this gift and seeking to understand what it's all about and how to use it. They often feel intimidated by it. It requires some assembly, and its instructions are hard to comprehend sometimes. How does the Bible fit together anyway? What does this ancient Book have to say to us who are looking toward the twenty-first century? Will taking the time and energy to understand its instructions and to fit it all together really help you and me?

Yes. Yes. Without a shred of doubt.

The *Spirit-Filled Life Bible Discovery Guide* series is designed to help you unwrap, assemble, and enjoy all God has for you in the pages of Scripture. It will focus your time and energy on the books of the Bible, the people and places they describe, and the themes and life applications that flow thick from its pages like honey oozing from a beehive.

So you can get the most out of God's Word, this series has a number of helpful features:

  WORD WEALTH

"WORD WEALTH" provides definitions of key terms.

BEHIND THE SCENES

"BEHIND THE SCENES" supplies information about cultural practices, doctrinal disputes, business trades, etc.

AT A GLANCE

"AT A GLANCE" features helpful maps and charts.

BIBLE EXTRA

"BIBLE EXTRA" will guide you to other resources that will enable you to glean more from the Bible's wealth.

PROBING THE DEPTHS

"PROBING THE DEPTHS" will explain controversial issues raised by particular lessons and cite Bible passages and other sources to help you come to your own conclusions.

FAITH ALIVE

The "FAITH ALIVE" feature will help you see and apply the Bible to your day-to-day needs.

The only resources you need to complete and apply these study guides are a heart and mind open to the Holy Spirit, a prayerful attitude, and a pencil and a Bible. Of course, you may draw upon other sources, but these study guides are comprehensive enough to give you all you need to gain a good, basic understanding of the Bible book being covered and how you can apply its themes and counsel to your life.

A word of warning, though. By itself, Bible study will not transform your life. It will not give you power, peace, joy, comfort, hope, and a number of other gifts God longs for you to unwrap and enjoy. Through Bible study, you will grow in your understanding of the Lord, His kingdom and your place in it, but you must be sure to rely on the Holy Spirit to guide your study and your application of the Bible's truths. He, Jesus promised, was sent to teach us "all things" (John 14:26; cf. 1 Cor. 2:13). Bathe your study time in prayer, asking the Spirit of God to illuminate the text, enlighten your mind, humble your will, and comfort your heart. He will never let you down.

My prayer and goal for you is that as you unwrap and begin to explore God's Book for living His way, the Holy Spirit will fill every fiber of your being with the joy and power God longs to give all His children. So read on. Be diligent. Stay open and submissive to Him. You will not be disappointed. He promises you!

Lesson 1/Facing Down Identity Fears

Basil walked silently through the streets of Caesarea. The future was uncertain, yet his mind was at peace. He had been called before the Roman prefect to answer for his preaching against the Arian teaching that Jesus the Son was created by the Father and inferior to Him. The emperor approved that teaching. *What would he face?*, Basil wondered. *Banishment? Death?* The future was uncertain, yet this bishop knew that he must hold to the teaching of Scripture: Jesus Christ was God and not a created being.

As he entered the hall where the prefect, Domitius Modustus, awaited to question him, Basil noticed two guards and a centurion stationed to one side. Was he to be arrested? He approached the seat of the prefect. Modestus questioned Basil about his teaching, and Basil simply replied that he could not give divine worship to any being other than God. "Then Modestus began to threaten and asked Basil if he wasn't afraid.

'Why should I be afraid? What can happen to me?'

'What can happen to you? You can lose your property and be banished. Torture. Death.'

'Try something else,' said Basil imperturbably. 'These things don't worry me.'"[1]

That episode is one of my favorite stories of courage. I can picture Basil standing there yawning as Modestus threatens him. "These things don't worry me." That steadfastness and courage, along with his faithful teaching and upright lifestyle, earned Basil the designation of Saint Basil the Great.

Paul too was a man of great courage. He faced persecution and death repeatedly for the sake of the gospel. Yet Paul was not without his own fears. "I was with you in weakness, in fear, and in much trembling" (1 Cor. 2:3).

"For we do not want you to be ignorant, brethren, of our trouble which came to us in Asia: that we were burdened beyond measure, above strength, so that we despaired even of life" (2 Cor. 1:8).

Galatians is known as one of the great epistles of faith, but it does not ignore fear. In our study, we will examine what Paul, the apostle of great faith, has to say about his own fears—and ours.

THE SETTING OF GALATIANS

The churches of Galatia were established during Paul's first missionary journey and included the churches of Antioch in Pisidia, Iconium, Lystra, and Derbe. These churches, being the firstfruits of Paul's ministry, were dear to him. In Galatia, Paul had begun his ministry to the Gentiles, and had established his doctrine of salvation by faith without works of the Law.

 AT A GLANCE

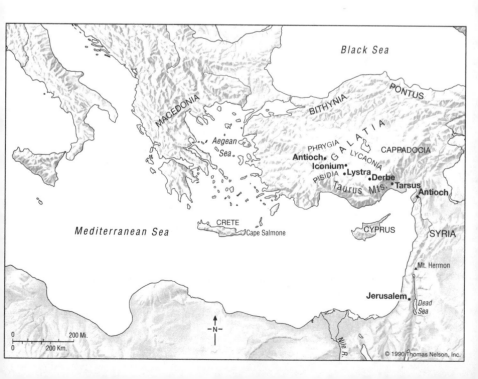

Yet other teachers had followed Paul. These teachers, known as Judaizers, taught that Gentiles had to be circumcised and turn to the Law as well as accepting Jesus as their Savior. In addition, they attacked Paul in two particular ways: 1) they claimed that his apostleship was either inauthentic or secondary to that of the original apostles, and 2) they attacked Paul's character, claiming that he was just preaching what people wanted to hear in order to obtain a following.

⚔ WORD WEALTH

Apostles, *apostolos.* A special messenger, a delegate, one commissioned for a particular task or role, one who is sent forth with a message. In the New Testament the word denotes both the original twelve disciples and prominent leaders outside the Twelve. Marvin Vincent records three features of an apostle: 1) one who had a visible encounter with the resurrected Christ; 2) one who plants churches; 3) one who functions in the ministry with signs, wonders, and miracles.[3]

Look in the book of Acts to find texts which illustrate the three features of an apostle in Paul's life.

1.

2.

3.

It is apparent that Paul fulfilled the role of an apostle, yet in his lifetime he continually battled with the Judaizers. In Galatians, one of the earliest of Paul's letters, he is particularly direct in answering their accusations.

Read Galatians 1:1–10. What specific statements does Paul make which relate to the two attacks of the Judaizers?

What statements does Paul make which relate to the features of an apostle listed above?

Paul was facing a problem which we all face: a fear regarding identity. Identity fear strikes us as it struck Paul—with a two-pronged attack. Attacks on identity are either suggestions that one *is* something that he is not, or it is the lack of recognition of what one truly is. In Paul's case the Judaizers were saying he was a man-pleaser (which he wasn't), and he was not an authentic apostle (which he was).

What fears do you face regarding your identity?

One difference we must note between ourselves and the apostle is the motivation behind our wish to establish or affirm our identity. Frequently, we wish people to recognize us and affirm us for selfish reasons. Paul, however, was supremely concerned for the Galatians themselves. His solution to the problems and questions which had arisen concerning his own identity was a firm and bold defense of his preaching and apostleship. Let us examine Paul's defense and see what he stresses as the answer to fears or questions about identity.

PAUL'S APOSTLESHIP

In Paul's answer to his opponents he stresses his source—not just his own roots in Judaism, but his ultimate source for both his message and his mission.

Read Galatians 1:11—2:10 and respond to the following items:

Paul stresses that the gospel he preached was not of human origin. List three ways this is stressed in this passage.

1.

2.

3.

What statements does Paul make emphasizing his call to the Gentiles?

What was the source or origin of Paul's message and call? List references.

 PROBING THE DEPTHS

Galatians chapters 1 and 2 are primarily a defense of Paul's apostleship, but they also give us a wealth of important biographical information about the apostle. These chapters can be correlated with Paul's movements in Acts to give us a fuller picture of his life.

Paul made five visits to Jerusalem after his conversion, according to Acts. These visits are listed in the following chart.

Paul's Post-conversion Visits to Jerusalem

Visit	Ref. in Acts
1. Saul's Post-conversion Visit	9:26–30
2. The Famine Visit	11:27–30
3. The Jerusalem Council	15:1–29
4. After the Second Missionary Journey	18:22
5. The Visit of his Arrest	21:15—23:35

Correlating these visits with Paul's account in Galatians is not a simple matter, and there are differences of opinion about which of the Acts visits correspond to the visits mentioned in Galatians.

There is general agreement that Paul's visit mentioned in Galatians 1:18–24 is the Post-conversion Visit. In Acts, Luke does not mention that three years passed. In fact, if we only had the record of Acts we might think that the Post-conversion Visit was very soon after Paul's conversion. But there is no reason to think that Luke and Paul are referring to different visits.

The identity of the visit Paul refers to in Galatians 2:1–10, however, is a source of much dispute. Scholarly opinion is divided on whether that visit is the Famine Visit or the Jerusalem Council. One of the key points in favor of the Galatians 2 visit being the Famine Visit is that the Jerusalem Council gave an authoritative decision on the relationship of the Gentiles to the Law and circumcision. This is a key subject in Galatians, yet Paul makes no allusion to the decision of the Council. Therefore, many believe that Paul wrote Galatians before the Jerusalem Council, and the visit in Galatians 2 is the Famine Visit.

A key argument against the Galatians 2 visit being the Famine Visit is an argument concerning time. Paul says there was a three-year gap from his conversion until his first visit to Jerusalem and fourteen years until the Galatians 2 visit. If these are consecutive time periods, then it was seventeen years from Paul's conversion until the Galatians 2 visit. The Jerusalem Council occurred in about A.D. 49–50 and seventeen years prior would put Paul's conversion at about A.D. 32–33 which itself is not long after the Passion and Resurrection of the Lord. To make the Galatians 2 visit the Famine Visit requires the addition of the First Missionary Journey before A.D. 49–50, and the timing simply does not work out.

More details on these two views can be found in the Introduction to Galatians in Appendix I.

THE SOURCE OF CONFIDENCE

We see how Paul boldly defended his preaching and his calling against the attacks of the Judaizers. He confidently asserted the truth of his message and the authenticity of his calling. But what does that mean to us? Do we depend on rhetorical powers to establish our identity? Is our confidence based on ourselves or how well we can argue our position? No, we must look again at Paul's source—the source of his message, the source of his confidence, and the source of his identity.

Read Galatians 2:11–21, and note especially the words live, life, and lives.

Why was Paul upset with Peter?

Who else was involved in Peter's error?

How is Peter living according to Paul? What is the significance of that statement?

The Law and faith are frequently contrasted throughout Galatians. List some distinctions Paul makes between the Law and faith in this passage.

Why must justification come by faith?

Who is the root of Paul's identity in verse 20? On what basis is the identification made?

The issue of identity is an issue about how you live, and how you live will be determined by the source from which you draw your life. Paul could say that the life he lived, he lived by faith in Jesus. Ultimately, Paul could be more concerned about the Galatians than about himself because he had already died— Christ now lived in him. We must see that Jesus Christ is both our identity and the solution to our fears regarding identity. Let us look further.

Read again Galatians 2:14–21.

What is the result of works of the Law?

If the Law is unfruitful in restoring men to God, how does justification come?

In verse 20, what figure does Paul use to indicate the extent to which our identities are lost in Christ's identity?

In verse 21, What is the basis for our justification through the work of Christ?

Why does Paul say that Christ died in vain if righteousness were available through the Law?

Paul here emphasizes that our identity is in Christ. Our identity does not come through our own efforts, but is rooted in Christ. In fact, Paul says we should identify so thoroughly with Christ that our own identity can be said to be dead. In other passages Paul also speaks of our total subservience to the Lord.

Read the following passages and comment on how they call you to submission to Christ.

Romans 6:3, 4

Romans 12:1, 2

Colossians 2:20—3:11

2 Timothy 2:3, 4

The point of all these passages is that our own life, identity, goals, and will are to be offered willingly to Christ. And if we are His servants, then our obedience to Him, not our reputation before man, is to be the object of our striving. In Philippians, Paul says it best,

"Brethren, I do not count myself to have apprehended; but one thing I do, forgetting those things which are behind and reaching forward to those things which are ahead, I press toward the goal for the prize of the upward call of God in Christ Jesus." (Phil. 3:13, 14).

FAITH ALIVE

That final prize, for which Paul was willing to lose all, is nothing less than to know Him and to be conformed to His death so that we might attain the final resurrection.

What do you see as being important parts of your own identity?

Are these elements of your identity submitted to Jesus Christ?

In what practical way are you demonstrating that your identity is in the Lord Jesus Christ?

It is a continual challenge to live in submission. Someone said that the problem with a living sacrifice is that it keeps crawling off the altar. Yet it is in submission to Christ that we find out who we truly are, and that brings freedom unbounded.

1. Donald Attwater, *Saints of the East,* (New York: P. J. Kenedy & Sons, 1963), ©1995

Lesson 2/Facing Down Fears Leading to Conformity

On the playground of an old elementary school in the heart of Los Angeles a group of third-graders engaged in a heated argument over the finer points of handball regulations. Several of the boys peppered their statements with "adult vocabulary" which had best remain unprinted. One youngster felt uneasy about that kind of talk, yet he wanted to fit in with his peers. His parents had never given him a list of "bad words," but he knew that that manner of speaking was wrong.

However, to fit in with his peers, and particularly to be like the leader of the group, he joined in the argument with all the gusto and swearing displayed by the other boys. This compromise in his way of talking did not stop there. It continued . . . until his parents found out. I don't remember the circumstances surrounding their discovery of his newly expanded vocabulary, but I remember the results well! You see, I was the third-grader who had learned to argue "like an adult." But when my parents found out, my methods of argument were significantly altered.

A little boy using bad words may seem like a humorous and almost quaint example of peer pressure, but that could have been just the beginning of a slippery slope of compromise had it not been corrected. We all have heard of people who, through peer pressure and compromise, fell into drugs, or sexual sin, or gang violence. Furthermore, we can each remember compromises of which we are ashamed.

Compromise due to peer pressure is essentially a fear-response. We fear what others will think of us, or we fear rejection. Although the issues involved in compromise may change, the root cause remains the same, so it is not surprising that we find the same problem in Galatians. In fact, we will look at two examples of fear-induced compromise.

PETER AND PEER PRESSURE

Peter is one of everyone's favorite personalities. You can't help but love the guy! As a disciple, he had his foot in his mouth more often than his fork, and his degree of bravado seemed matched only by his degree of failure. Yet Jesus' patient tutelage, and the empowering presence of the Holy Spirit, made him into one of the pillars of the early church.

Yet even the power of the Spirit did not make Peter infallible. (This should be a comfort to us!) In Galatians, Paul tells about a time when he had to confront and correct Peter.

Read Galatians 2:11–21.

Why did Paul oppose Peter?

Why did Peter withdraw from the Gentiles?

When did Peter withdraw from the Gentiles?

Of what was Peter afraid?

Peter was clearly intimidated by the Jewish Christians who came from James. The controversy over Gentile acceptance in the church was heating up, and many of the more traditional Jews accepted James as their leader. Peter's freedom to eat with the Gentiles could easily be misunderstood by the Jews, and the Jews were Peter's primary sphere of ministry. Peter feared that misunderstanding could be detrimental to his work for the Lord. However, he failed to recognize that his compromise with the Law was detrimental to the purity of the gospel.

PROBING THE DEPTHS

James

James was a key figure in the early church. He is alluded to here in Galatians, and he was one of the leaders involved in the Jerusalem Council. But who is he and what is his connection to the Galatians?

First, James was not the son of Zebedee, the apostle John's brother. We are told in Acts 12 that James the brother of John was killed by Herod. The indications from the Bible and church history are that this James was the half-brother of Jesus, and also the writer of the book of James. (John 7:3, Acts 1:14, Matt. 13:55, Jude 1).

James was heavily involved with the Jews of Judea. He cared deeply for his countrymen and prayed fervently for their salvation. It was his practice to adhere strictly to Jewish customs as a means of witnessing to the Jews around him. He was probably a stricter Jew than those he lived among, and even among the non-Christians he had a reputation for being righteous.

This emphasis on practice can be observed easily in the book of James, and some—both in his time and since—have been confused by his doctrine of works. But James was never confused. The position he took in the Jerusalem Council clearly shows that he knew that works were not the source of salvation, but rather the fruit of salvation.

It is likely that the books of James and Galatians were both written prior to the Jerusalem Council. These writings show us the differences in emphasis that led to controversy, but there is no indication that Paul and James were ever personally in conflict.

The question of eating with Gentiles involved Jewish ritual. The Jews would not eat with the Gentiles because they were "unclean." Questions about Jewish religious law, how it was to be observed, and how much the Gentiles had to observe were critical questions in the first decades of the church's life. In A.D. 49 or 50 the leaders of the church met at Jerusalem in order to deal specifically with the question of Gentiles coming to Christ.

 BEHIND THE SCENES

The Jerusalem Council—Acts 15

In Acts 15 we are told of a very important event in the life of the early church. The Jerusalem Council was critically important for at least two reasons: 1) The Council determined that a Gentile could become a Christian without submitting to the ceremonial regulations of Judaism. This decision prevented Christianity from remaining just a Jewish sect. 2) The methodology by which this decision was made established a precedent which guided early Christianity. Over the first several centuries a number of councils were called to deal decisively with important matters of doctrine and heresy. Doctrines concerning the Trinity, the dual nature of the Lord Jesus Christ, and the establishment of the canon of Scripture were among the issues agreed upon in the great ecumenical councils of the church.

As stated in the last lesson, the Jerusalem Council also has particular significance for the book of Galatians. The purpose for writing Galatians was to answer the very same issues which were being settled in the Jerusalem Council. In addition, the dating of Galatians is primarily influenced by two issues: whether Galatians was written to north Galatia or south Galatia, and whether Galatians was written before or after the Jerusalem Council.

Peter caved in to peer pressure on this occasion. The ironic thing we see here is that the "peer pressure" in this case was tending toward a more legalistic lifestyle. We generally think of peer pressure as something which leads us to compromise a standard rather than go back to a more rigorous stan-

dard. But Paul recognized the compromise for what it was—
nothing less than a compromise of the entire gospel!

How was Peter's action a compromise of the gospel?

THE GALATIANS' COMPROMISE

As we have seen, Paul was vehement about defending the
gospel he preached. He vigorously defended the gospel against
his opponents, and he even confronted Peter for the sake of
the gospel of grace. In this epistle, Paul likewise confronts the
Galatians, for the Galatians were in danger of making the same
error that Peter made, and for much the same reason.

Read Galatians 3:1–14

Paul introduces this part of the letter with a series of questions. Restate the main questions Paul asks and answer them.

What was the main error the Galatians were making?

Why do you think the Galatians were turning back to the
Law?

What does Paul state the Galatians have received?

By what two means is God working in the Galatians?

Who is seen as our prime example, and why?

Why are we under a curse?

How is the curse on us removed?

What is the result of the removal of the curse?

The Galatians had begun to drift away from the gospel of grace and were turning back to works. This probably seemed a logical step: the Judaizers seemed so holy and sincere. In addition, they had scriptural arguments, and many others were following their teaching.

But Paul, in a strong rebuke, cuts through all the nonsense, and his key point is worthy of attention.

> *"Did you receive the Spirit by the works of the law, or by the hearing of faith?" (Gal. 3:2).*

The Galatians had been touched by the Spirit. They had begun a new life through faith in Christ and by the power of the Spirit. In addition, they had seen the miraculous power of the Spirit working in their midst. Their personal experience of the working of the Spirit was part of Paul's argument against the doctrines of the Judaizers. God, who supplies the Spirit, had done so in response to their faith, not their works.

It is important to note the emphasis which Paul puts on their experience in the Spirit. Paul is arguing that the division lies between the Spirit and the Law: the Spirit is received by faith and the Law is accomplished by works. The traditional view of Galatians sees the dichotomy between faith and works, yet it has usually missed the underlying division between the

Law and the Spirit. Yet this division between the Law and the Spirit is crucial to Paul's argument. The Galatians have become part of the people of God because they have received the Spirit, not because they have been circumcised. Furthermore, they live in the Spirit doing the works of the Spirit; their life is not controlled by the observance of the Law.

Paul's appeal to the Galatians' experience in the Spirit is seen more clearly if we look closer at his statement in verse 4: "Have you suffered so many things in vain . . .?" Some translations of the Bible render the verb "suffered" as "experienced." The reason for this difference is that Paul uses that particular word (*pascho*) elsewhere in his letters to mean "suffer," but the usual meaning of the word is "experience." Thus, there is a division among scholars regarding the preferable translation. But if we take the usual connotation of the word, we can see that Paul is appealing directly to their experience in the Spirit.

This experience is both past and present. Paul speaks clearly of his initial preaching of the gospel in Galatians 3:1 and to their receiving of the Spirit at that time in 3:2. But he is also making the important point that their experience of the Spirit is continuing. God is still working miracles and supplying the Spirit in the present—now (Gal. 3:5).

WORD WEALTH

Supplies, *epichoregeo.* A combination of *epi,* intensive, and *choregeo,* "to defray the expenses of a chorus." The word thus means to supply fully or abundantly, generously provide what is needed, cover the costs completely. It is used with the strong connotation of great and free generosity. Paul is chiding the Galatians for regressing to the beggarly elements of legalism, which he contrasts with the abounding surplus of God's provision through grace.[1]

We likewise need to recognize that our experiences and the testimony of what God has done in our lives are worthy to be part of the foundation of our faith. God is still supplying the Spirit and working miracles through faith, and these experiences are supposed to be edifying. They are part of our relationship with God.

In my teenage years, I did some of the questioning that many do. I decided that I needed to analyze my beliefs and determine if my belief in God was well-founded. Through subsequent years I have learned about many arguments for the existence of God, but in my teenage years I really did not need them. I determined that I could not question God's existence because I had seen and experienced too much of God's work to seriously question His existence.

Paul knew that the personal experiences of the Galatians were important to the establishment of their faith; however, Paul did not leave their faith based on subjective experiences. He went directly to the Word of God to explain and give example of justification by faith.

Look again at Galatians 3:5–14. What are the key points in Paul's explanation of justification by faith?

PEER PRESSURE AND FEAR PRESSURE

The Galatians desired to be accepted; it was typical peer pressure. Peter was afraid of what others might think; it was typical fear pressure. But both cases led to a compromise of what had been learned, and experienced, and believed.

Peter had walked with Jesus. He had learned from the Master and had seen the miracles. He had even seen the resurrected Lord. He knew that "we ought to obey God rather than men." (Acts 5:29). Yet he needed a reminder.

The Galatians also had learned much and seen much. The initial work of Paul among the Galatians is recorded in Acts 13 and 14. Let us examine the experience of the Galatians and discover some of the things they had learned.

Read Acts 13:16–41.

This sermon is recognized as a pattern of the way Paul presented the gospel. As such, we can be sure that these basic ideas were taught to all the Galatian churches during that first missionary journey.

What is Paul's purpose in verses 16 to 23? Why does he begin the sermon that way?

What is the main point in this opening part of Paul's sermon?

What is Paul's emphasis in verses 23 to 31?

The final portion of the sermon is the proclamation. What are the three key declarations Paul makes?

What statement is made which most directly bears on the message of the letter to the Galatians?

Paul's sermon is a masterwork of communication. He got the attention and interest of his audience by connecting his message to them. Paul spoke of Jewish history. This not only piqued their interest, it also showed that his message was grounded in historical fact. He then went on to give the crux of his gospel: Jesus came, He died, and He rose again. But Paul did not leave it there. He went back to Scripture to interpret the significance of the message. Perhaps the most significant thing Paul said in relation to our present study was "by Him everyone who believes is justified from all things from which you could not be justified by the law of Moses" (Acts 13:39). This statement is a direct parallel to the message of Galatians.

Paul also taught them that following the gospel would not

always be accepted and that "we must through many tribulations enter the kingdom of God." (Acts 14:22). Following the gospel does have a cost; it does require sacrifice. Paul was stoned and left for dead at Lystra, so the Galatians knew firsthand what the cost could be. Yet they, like Peter, needed a reminder.

Thus we see that Paul used directness in dealing with the results of fear-induced compromise; he was not at all timid in correction. Yet Paul also continually went back to the source. We saw in the first lesson how Paul went back to the source to answer fears regarding identity. Likewise, here he goes to the source for correcting compromise.

Just as our identification with Christ is the key to our identity, so also the force which animates your life does not find its source in the world or in your peers but "the just shall live by faith" (Gal. 3:11). As Paul led the Galatians back to their beginnings (Gal. 3:3), so we need to rediscover the beginnings of our faith. The Holy Spirit, working through His own gentle power and the power of the Word, brought us to faith in Christ. This faith is the source of our courage to stand in Christ. It is a faith based on the work of the Spirit in our lives, made more secure by being grounded in the eternal Word of God.

 FAITH ALIVE

What experiences has God used in your life to edify your faith?

What Scriptures or lessons from the Word has God particularly used in your life?

The balance between our personal experience and our learning of the Bible is not easily achieved. Many people find the present working of the Spirit so exciting that they become totally oriented toward experience. These people can be deceived easily because their eyes are on the signs rather than on what the signs point to.

On the other hand, there are those who study with rigor. They know their doctrines backward and forward and they are ready to test those who are apostles and are not, and find them to be liars (Rev. 2:2). But like the church of Ephesus, these people have forgotten that God wants to have a relationship with us. The church *is* an army, but we are not continually in boot camp.

The balance is found in faith. Faith believes and studies the Word, yet sees that the limits of our comprehension are not the endpoints of the Spirit's work. Faith goes beyond both experience and teaching into relationship with God.

1. *Spirit-Filled Life Bible* (Nashville, TN: Thomas Nelson Publishers, 1991), 1776, "Word Wealth: Gal. 3:5, supplies."

Lesson 3/Facing Down Fear of Loss

In 1987 Bill and Lynn were living in a two-bedroom apartment just off Sherman Way in Van Nuys, California. Their apartment was about ten miles west of the Hollywood-Burbank Airport, and one of the flight paths to the airport went right down Sherman Way. As a result, airplanes were going over their apartment on a regular basis.

For many people this would be a disturbing fact, and it was for Bill. He had a wife and baby daughter who were home all day and, although there were many other things which posed a greater chance of danger than a plane crash, the sound of planes passing overhead was a regular reminder that he could easily lose what he held most dear.

God helped Bill to overcome these fears. Here is Bill's story about how he learned to trust God with the safety of his family.

"One day, as I was on my way to work, I was talking to the Lord about my worries. 'God,' I said, 'what if there was a plane crash and I wasn't there?'

"He answered my question with a question, 'What if you were there?'

"I had to laugh at myself. What could I do if I was at home and a Boeing 727 fell out of the sky? Stand on the roof and catch it? The Lord gently reminded me that I have very little control over most things. This could be a frightening thought except that God watches over us. That day I learned that I am far better off leaving my family's safety in God's hands than worrying about it myself. He can control all those things which I cannot."

Fear of loss is something we all face at one time or another. It may be fear of losing loved ones—as in Bill's case, or it may be the fear that all you have worked for will be lost. Job said, "That which I feared most has come upon me," so apparently he suffered from that sort of fear.

PAUL'S FEAR OF LOSS

In Galatians we see Paul suffering from that sort of fear. He had worked hard and suffered much in establishing the Galatian churches, yet it looked like everything was going to be lost. "I am afraid for you, lest I have labored for you in vain." (Gal. 4:11).

Paul's fears were not without grounds. Read Galatians 4:8–20 and list the reasons Paul was afraid for the Galatians.

Why did Paul initially preach the gospel in Galatia?

How does Paul describe his acceptance among the Galatians?

What is meant by the statement "they want to exclude you," (4:17), and who are THEY?

In verse 20 Paul says he would like to change his tone; what expressions does Paul use in chapters 3 and 4 which show his intensity of emotion?

Paul's fear that the Galatians were turning back to legalistic teaching is amply shown by the emotion with which he appeals to the Galatians. He did not want to lose the fruit of his first Gentile mission. Yet we are told that his initial plans did not include the Galatians, but that he went into Galatia because of some physical problem.

BEHIND THE SCENES

Paul's infirmity

From the book of Acts we know that Paul and Barnabas preached first in Cyprus and then arrived on the south coast of Asia Minor. The record of Acts tells us nothing of an infirmity, but Paul and Barnabas did go quickly into the region of Galatia with no recorded missionary activity on the coast. That fact, along with the Galatian record, suggests that Paul did come down with some kind of ailment, and commentators suggest that they traveled inland believing that the fresh air of the higher elevations would be restorative.

There are three main theories regarding the nature of this infirmity, but they are all speculative—based only on small bits of evidence.

1. The disease was a malarial type of fever. Some commentators believe that Paul may have contracted a fever in the coastal lowlands and went into Galatia to get out of the diseased environment and recover.

2. Paul's infirmity was epilepsy. This correlates better with the suggestion in Galatians 4:14 that the trial was one for which the Galatians may have been expected to reject Paul. In the first century epilepsy was thought to be the result of an evil spirit, so people would avoid epileptics. The verb "reject" in verse 14 "(Greek, *ekptuo*) is literally 'to spit out,' which some commentators take to be a reference to the custom of spitting in the direction of an epileptic to avert the influence of the evil spirit supposedly residing in him."[1]

3. Paul suffered from some kind of eye disease. This, too, could explain the suggestion that the Galatians might have rejected Paul. It is also suggested as the explanation of Paul's statement that the Galatians "would have plucked out your own eyes and given them to me" (4:15).

Although Paul did not intend to preach in Galatia, it was providentially arranged by God that the Galatians would hear the gospel. Recognizing God's hand, Paul was zealous to establish God's work. This too should be a lesson to us. We may find ourselves in situations or with responsibilities that we did not plan. However, we must recognize that God's planning is more intricate and subtle than ours. If God arranges an assignment for us, we should fulfill it to the best of our abilities with God's help.

Having acknowledged that God had willed that the Galatians hear the gospel, and expressing his fear that the Galatians would fall from the gospel, Paul goes on to describe his solution: he will labor in birth until Christ is formed in them (4:19).

 WORD WEALTH

Formed, *morphoo:* to form. *Schema* and *morphoo* are in bold contradistinction. *Schema* (English "scheme") signifies external form or outer appearance. *Morphoo* and *morphe,* its related noun, refer to internal reality. Galatians 4:19 speaks of a change in character, becoming conformed to the character of Christ in actuality, not merely in semblance.[2]

It was Paul's desire to see a true, internal, heart-level change in the Galatians, and he knew that change had to be the work of the Lord. So how was this change to take place?

CHRIST IN YOU

Just as the Galatians needed to have Christ formed in them, so we also need the heart-level change which indicates our own conformance into the image of Christ. This is a work of grace—we cannot change ourselves. But we must cooperate with this work. Reread Galatians 3:1–14 and answer the following questions.

What statements are made which indicate the work of God in the transformation of one's life?

What statements are made which indicate one's own cooperation with the work of God?

This passage clearly states that the_____of the Law are useless, but God works by_____.

In this passage Paul is speaking primarily about justification and the fact that justification comes only through faith. Yet we must take to heart the message of verse 3. "Having begun in the Spirit, are you now being made perfect by the flesh?" God uses the same power to continue His work that He used to begin His work. We were saved by grace through faith, and we continue to be saved—that is, conformed into the likeness of Christ Jesus—by grace through faith.

 WORD WEALTH

Faith, *pistis:* Conviction, confidence, trust, belief, reliance, trustworthiness, and persuasion. In the New Testament setting, *pistis* is the divinely implanted principle of inward confidence, assurance, trust, and reliance in God and all that He says. The word sometimes denotes the object or content of belief (Acts 6:7; 14:22; Gal. 1:23)[3]

What is the best description for faith as the word is used in Galatians 3:1–14?

What was the object of Abraham's faith?

Thus we see that Christ is formed in us by faith. We must cooperate with the work of the Spirit, for if we resist, He cannot work in our lives. Yet the power to be changed into the image and likeness of Christ does not originate with us.

In addition to faith being necessary for us to become like Christ, we need to rely on the promises of God.

Read Galatians 3:15–18; Genesis 12:1–9; and Genesis 17:1–14.

What promises were made to Abraham?

How do these promises apply to us?

From the passages in Genesis, list at least two ways that the covenant was confirmed.

What is the main point of Paul's argument in verses 15–18?

So the promises which God makes cannot be annulled. The Law—even though it was given by God—could not annul the promises. Therefore, nothing in your own life, nothing in your own experience, nothing of your own actions can annul the promises which were given by God in Christ and confirmed by the death and resurrection of Jesus Christ our Lord.

Look up the following verses and briefly summarize what they say about your growing in His image.

Romans 8:11

2 Corinthians 3:18

Philippians 1:7

So we see that this growth toward the likeness of Christ is something that happens by faith—it is the work of the Spirit, not our efforts. It is sealed by the promises of God—progress will continue until the task is complete. But we cannot deny that it is a process. Growth of any kind requires time and comes in stages.

Examine Galatians 3:19—4:7 and answer these questions.

What illustration does Paul use to describe the function of the Law?

What was the result of the Law? What was the Law unable to provide?

What illustration does Paul use in describing the process of God's plan of redemption?

How can that illustration be applied to each of us individually?

Read Paul's illustration in Galatians 4:21–31.

What is Paul contrasting in his analogy?

Which part of the illustration applies to us?

According to this passage, what kind of children are we?

Compare and contrast this illustration with Paul's illustration in 4:1–7. What are some of the similarities?

What are some of the differences?

In what ways do both these illustrations show that our growth in Christ-likeness is a process?

Paul taught that Christ-likeness came by faith (*pistis*), by promise, and as a process. Seeing all three of these aspects is important. Faith tells us that we ourselves are not the source of power to change. Conformity into Christ's image is a result of our cooperation with the Holy Spirit's transformation. Additionally, we have the promises of God as a guarantee that His work will be accomplished. Just as a contractor will post a bond as a guarantee that the work will be done, God has given us the Holy Spirit, in addition to His promises, as our guarantee (Eph. 1:14). Therefore, we have confidence that God's work in us will be accomplished, but it still takes time—it is a process.

OUR FEARS ANSWERED

So Paul's fear of loss was answered by his teaching on the faith, and the promise, and the process of Christ being formed in us. Our own fear of loss can be answered according to the same pattern: faith, promise, process.

Faith

"Faith is the substance of things hoped for, the evidence of things not seen." (Heb. 11:1). That is probably the most oft-quoted definition of faith, and it is a good definition. However, sometimes we quote something so often that we stop thinking about its real meaning. Combine the idea stated in Hebrews 11:1 with the idea we discussed earlier: faith is God accomplishing His purpose, by His power, with our permission. The things which we want to take hold of by faith are grasped when we let go. Our own works do not accomplish His work.

Promise

God has promised us many things in His Word. Yet many people misunderstand His promises. We ought not treat the promises as though they are legally binding contracts—we cannot demand anything from God. Rather His promises are specific, concrete examples of His grace. God has made promises, and He will be true to His word, but not because He is under legal bondage. What an absurd thought: the Lord of all the universe bound by a contract. But His promises are gracious offers which He will not renege upon, for He cannot deny His own goodness, faithfulness, and love.

WORD WEALTH

Promise, *epangelia:* both a promise and the thing promised, an announcement with the special sense of promise, pledge, and offer. *Epangelia* tells what the promise from God is and then gives the assurance that the thing promised will be done. Second Corinthians 1:20 asserts, "For all the promises of God in Him are Yes, and in Him Amen, to the glory of God through us."[4]

So we can rely on His promises; our faith has a sure foundation. And our greatest assurance rests on the fact that "He who did not spare His own Son, but delivered Him up for us all, how shall He not with Him also freely give us all things?" (Rom. 8:32).

Process

The answering of our fears is a process. It seems that we overcome one fear only to be assailed by another. But in childlike faith we must continue to turn to God with our fears. Galatians 4:6, 7 tell us that the Spirit comes to us allowing us to call out to Abba Father. By this we know that we are no longer slaves, but sons. Romans 8:15 explicitly tells us that we are no longer slaves to fear, but have been adopted and can cry out "Abba Father." So the process of overcoming fear of loss, or any other fear, is to continually turn back to Abba Father. As our relationship with Him grows, so too will our trust in Him and our faith in His promises.

 FAITH ALIVE

What things do you need to put back in God's hands by faith?

What do you need to do to stop holding on to a fear and give it to God in faith?

What promises has God made concerning the things you are trusting Him with?

What promise have you seen God fulfill in the past?

Take a moment now to thank God for His past faithfulness and give your fears back to Him again.

1. *Spirit-Filled Life Bible* (Nashville, TN: Thomas Nelson Publishers, 1991), 1778, "Notes: Gal. 4:13–15."
2. Ibid., 1778, "Word Wealth, Gal.4:19, formed."
3. Ibid., 1492, "Word Wealth, Mark 11:22, faith."
4. Ibid., 1652, "Word Wealth, Acts 13:32, promise."

Lesson 4/Fears About Salvation

Are you or one you love at risk of Galatianitis? This condition afflicts millions of believers yearly. It was first diagnosed early in the life of the church and has never been eradicated fully. Throughout history there have been periodic outbreaks of epidemic proportions. In fact, one outbreak became so serious that it had to be treated with massive doses of Reformation.

Look for these early-warning signs of this serious condition: Have you ever fallen in sin and not asked immediately for forgiveness because you wanted to prove to God that you were serious about living right? Have you had something bad happen and figured you deserved it? Have you wondered if you were saved because you were not doing enough? Do you feel you need to work hard to stay saved? If you answered yes to any of the above questions, you may be at risk for Galatianitis. But take heart, there is an antidote.

The apostle Paul dealt with an early outbreak of this condition, and his diagnosis and treatment became standard. Thus the condition was named for that outbreak in the region of Galatia.

Paul found that believers suffering from this condition felt a need for works, had a tendency to turn back to old ways, and desired to conform to legalistic standards. His brilliant diagnosis found the root cause to be fears about one's salvation. In this case study we will see how Paul treated specific symptoms, as well as how he addressed the root cause.

THE NEED FOR WORKS

Periodically most of us feel we need to do something to earn or deserve our salvation. After all, we are told that nothing is free, and we have to work to get what we want out of life. Our salvation is surely the greatest and most valuable thing we have, so it just seems logical that we should do something to earn it.

The Galatians also felt a need to do something—to perform works for their salvation. Let us examine Galatians 3:10–18 and discover some signs of their problem.

What statements does Paul make which indicate that the Galatians were depending upon works?

What kind of works were the Galatians going back to?

Paul speaks of a blessing and a curse. What is the source of each?

We see here that the Galatians had turned back to the Law as a means of justification. However, Paul explains that the Law is a source of cursing, not blessing. God knows that man has an inborn desire to justify himself. This self-justification takes place either through making excuses or trying to earn forgiveness. On the one hand a man will say, "No, I really didn't do wrong"; on the other he will say, "Yes, I blew it, but I will make it up to you." Therefore, God gave the Law to respond to both of these expressions of self-justification.

In the Law God shows us that each and every one of us has done wrong, and He also shows us there is no way we can make it up to Him. This is why Paul says that the Law brings a curse: it tells us that we are inadequate and there is no way we can become adequate.

However, Paul did not just come and kick the crutches out from under the Galatians. He wanted the Galatians to know that their standing with God was on a much surer foundation than their own flimsy works. There is a changeless promise which reaches back prior to the Law.

In the passage we just read, to whom is the promise given?

How does Paul connect this promise with Christ?

Based on Galatians 3:10–18, what is the sure foundation of our salvation?

How did Christ remove the curse from us?

The work of Christ is the antidote to our own works. We must recognize the fallacy of depending upon ourselves. We cannot save ourselves, we cannot keep ourselves saved, and we cannot earn God's blessing. In fact, we need to go back and challenge our basic assumptions.

Contrary to the idea that nothing is free, we must see that our greatest possession is free. Furthermore, those things of greatest value to us we did not earn. Which one of us truly believes that he or she earned his or her spouse's love? Who earned their children? Families may be a lot of work, but we do not earn them in the same sense in which we earn a raise or a promotion. Our most valuable possessions are valuable precisely because we did not earn them, for what is earned can be replaced by our own efforts. The truly priceless things are freely given, yet irreplaceable.

Name some ways that God has blessed you with things which you did not earn.

TURNING BACK TO OLD WAYS

The second symptom which Paul addresses is turning back to old ways. We all learn by example, and it is natural for us to look back to our old examples to find direction. In Galatians 4:8–11 we see Paul addressing this particular problem as manifested in the Galatians.

In Galatians 4:8–11 what old ways are drawing the Galatians back?

Does the statement regarding observation of days and seasons refer to Jewish observations, or something pagan? Why do you think so?

What do you think the phrase "weak and beggarly elements" means?

Paul was worried about the Galatians because they were turning back to their old patterns and examples to find answers. In the case of the Galatians these old patterns were both Jewish and pagan. Acts 14 tells us that Paul began his preaching in the synagogue, where he preached to Jews and God-fearing Gentiles (Acts 13:16, 42, 43). On the second Sabbath, "almost the whole city came together to hear the word of God" (Acts 13:44). In addition to the Jews and God-fearers who came to Christ, many of Paul's initial converts were probably from a pagan background.

This understanding of the background of Paul's converts is important because it influences how we understand the phrase "weak and beggarly elements." This, in turn, influences how we understand what Paul is saying in this passage. Let's look more closely at this phrase.

PROBING THE DEPTHS

The term "elements" is the Greek word *stoicheia* from which we get the word "stoichiometry," which relates to the proportions with which the chemical elements react and form compounds. In the first century it also referred to the elements of earth, air, fire, and water, but it could also refer to the basic principles of anything—even the alphabet.

Paul used the word twice in Galatians (4:3, 9) and twice in Colossians (2:8, 20). Commentators are divided on the precise connotation we should give to Paul's use. Some believe that he referred to pre-Christian religious experiences—either Jewish or pagan. Others believe it relates particularly to the observance of the Law. Others believe he is speaking of people being subject to the influence of demonic spirits prior to their coming to Jesus.

Look up the four references cited above and consider what meaning should be given to *stoicheia.* You may also wish to consult a good commentary on Galatians, such as *Mastering the New Testament,* volume 8, by M. D. Dunnam; the *Word Biblical Commentary,* volume 41, by R. I. Longenecker; or the *Tyndale New Testament Commentaries,* volume 9, by R. A. Cole.

We see that Paul referred to the prior religious experience of the Galatians as "weak and beggarly," regardless of whether its origin was in Judaism or in paganism. We must not think that Paul considered Judaism and paganism as equivalent. He

is very clear in a number of writings—including Galatians—
that the Law fulfilled a purpose in God's plan. In contrast to
that, Paul, in Romans 1, speaks of paganism as a downward
spiral into all manner of wickedness. So Paul was not saying
that all the Galatians came from a similar background, but that,
whatever their background, it was inadequate and they could
not go back for answers.

To find new answers the Galatians had to look to new
examples, and Paul gives two.

Read Galatians 4:12–31.

What two examples are the Galatians given?

In what ways does Paul commend the Galatians?

In what ways does Paul want the Galatians to imitate him?

What parallels can be drawn between us and Isaac?

Here we see that Paul was emphasizing a new example
and a new source. Paul himself was the example. Here he
urges, "become like me" (4:12). In another letter he says,
"Imitate me, just as I also imitate Christ" (1 Cor. 11:1). Paul
was not afraid to urge people to follow him because he knew
where he was going.

We also see that Paul spoke of a new source. We are no
longer under the bondage of the Law; that is, we no longer
need to seek acceptance on the basis of works. We are called
"children of promise" (4:28). We have been accepted on the

basis of God's promises, and now we also live on the basis of God's promises. It is no longer our works, but Christ's work, which has brought us into relationship with God.

Conformity

In Paul's dealings with the Galatians his strongest rebuke came in response to their tendency to conform. We saw in Paul's confrontation with Peter that Paul had a very low tolerance for conformity. Yet at the same time, he desired conformity. Look at the following passage and note what Paul says against and in favor of conformity.

Read Galatians 4:16–20.

Who desires the Galatians to conform to their standards?

What does Paul say is the result of conformity?

What does Paul say in favor of conformity?

In the following verses, what are we to be conformed to?

Romans 8:29

2 Corinthians 3:18

Ephesians 4:24

Philippians 3:10

Philippians 3:21

Conformity is not one-sided. Paul encouraged the Galatians not to conform to those who wished only to pad their religious credentials. Rather, our pattern is to be Jesus Christ our Lord. We are to conform to His death, to His image, and to His life. Our new life has its source in His resurrected life.

RELATIONSHIP WITH GOD

The crux of all these things is our relationship with God. It is in getting a clear picture of our relationship with God that we find the universal antidote to all the symptoms of Galatianitis.

List the different terms Paul uses in describing us in Galatians 3:26—4:7.

What are some of the differences between our relationship to God based on Law as opposed to our relationship based on adoption?

What further insights does Paul give us concerning sonship in Galatians 4:21–31?

Our adoption as sons and daughters of God is the new basis for our relationship with God. We no longer relate to God on a legal basis. Our works could never have brought us into right relationship with God, and they cannot keep us in right relationship with God. God has given His Son to secure our adoption, and He has given His Spirit to seal our adoption.

 ## FAITH ALIVE

Our salvation is assured. We know it is based on Christ's work. It is a new and living way; we must not turn back to the old ways. And our new relationship calls us to a new conformity. But beyond all these things, our standing is based on a relationship with God as our Father. We are adopted sons and daughters.

How does this view of your salvation affect your perspective?

What specific symptoms of Galatianitis can you address on the basis of this perspective?

Lesson 5/Freedom in the Spirit

On November 9, 1989, the Berlin Wall fell. That wall had been a symbol of oppression, a visible manifestation of the Iron Curtain. Hundreds had died trying to escape through its labyrinth of guards and booby traps. The ground bore blood and mines, and the barbed wire became a final resting place for many who yearned to breathe free. Its guards personified the menace of the Wall, and millions were separated from the hope of freedom by its whitewashed escarpment. And it fell. On that wonderful autumn day, it fell—amidst the cheering of millions.

In the weeks following that earth-shaking event the world would have been even more bewildered if the Germans had begun rebuilding the Wall. If the German people had said, "Yes, freedom is wonderful, but this just doesn't feel normal! We're used to the Wall," the world would have been stunned.

If we can understand that picture then we can understand how Paul felt in his dealings with the Galatians. The Lord Jesus had broken down the wall and brought the fabulous new hope of freedom from sin and the Law, and now the Galatians wanted to go back! It's enough to give an apostle a headache!

Yet we face the same problem. We have been freed from legalistic requirements; we cannot, and need not, try to earn our salvation. Yet we are easily swayed into legalistic lifestyles. We are freed from sin; we are no longer in bondage to the habits and lifestyles which we pursued in darkness. Yet we are even more easily swayed back into the sins we should be free of. We don't need to read Romans 7 to know that the flesh, our carnal nature, is still active within us.

In this lesson we will look at the freedom in the Spirit which is ours through faith in Christ. Paul is now finishing his answer to the question which he asked back in chapter 3:

"Having begun in the Spirit are you now being made perfect by the flesh?" (Gal. 3:3) Paul has answered with a resounding "No!" Now, he is wrapping up his argument by showing that the Spirit alone—not any work of the flesh—is all that is required for entry into life in Christ, and for continuing in Christ. The works of the flesh, both legalistic and licentious, are counterproductive. Let us look closer at Paul's concept of "the flesh" as seen in Galatians.

THE FLESH

Paul knew that dealing with the flesh was an ongoing process that began, not ended, when one came to repentance. He spoke of his own struggle with the flesh, and he frequently admitted that he had to subject himself to discipline in order to attain the prize for which he was striving. He told the Galatians that the Spirit and the flesh are at war. But before we drift into an unscriptural asceticism we need to clearly define what is meant by the word "flesh."

WORD WEALTH

Flesh, *sarx:* in its literal sense, *sarx* refers to the substance of the body, whether of animals or persons (1 Cor. 15:39; 2 Cor. 12:7). In its idiomatic use, the word indicates the human race or personhood (Matt. 24:22; 1 Pet. 1:24). In an ethical and spiritual sense, *sarx* is the lower nature of a person, the seat and vehicle of sinful desires (Rom. 7:25; Gal. 5:16, 17).[1]

Read the following Scriptures and determine what the word "flesh" means in each.

Acts 2:26

Romans 1:3

Romans 8:4

Galatians 1:16

Ephesians 5:29

Colossians 2:13

James 5:3

When Paul spoke of our war with the flesh he was not speaking of denying the physical body, but of putting to death that lower, carnal nature which dwells in each of us. This carnal nature has to be fought on two fronts. First, there are base, carnal desires which we fight against; discipline of our physical appetites *is* necessary. But a less obvious manifestation of the carnal nature is our tendency toward legalism. We may not follow a well-defined legal code, but whenever we think we have earned something, or have a right to something, we are not depending on grace, and we have given in to the legalistic tendencies of our carnal nature.

THE WORKS OF THE LAW

Paul addresses both aspects of our carnal nature: the works of the Law and the works of the flesh. But the more pressing problem in Galatia was their falling back into legalism. So it is to the works of the Law that Paul directs his first correction.

Read Galatians 5:1–15 and answer the following questions.

To what "yoke of bondage" is Paul referring in verse 1?

Why does Paul say that one who is circumcised needs to keep the whole Law? (See Gal. 3:10)

Read verses 5 and 6 and comment on our hope and the means by which we attain our hope.

What does Paul mean by saying, "A little leaven leavens the whole lump"?

Why would "the offense of the cross" cease if Paul preached circumcision? What is "the offense of the cross"?

How are we to use our freedom in Christ? How are we not to use it?

Paul speaks here of freedom from the Law. His references to circumcision and to the Judaizers clearly indicate that Paul is addressing the legalistic tendencies of some of the Galatians. Paul knew that we have a tendency to try to mix our own works into God's ways. Ever since Cain offered the fruit of his labor (Gen. 4), man has been trying to work his way back to God. Paul also knew that any allowance for works would result in a legalistic works program eventually displacing grace. Therefore, Paul's key argument throughout this entire letter is that the entry of the Spirit, and the continuing work of the Spirit within us, is the key to living our life in Christ. It is the foundation of our freedom in Christ.

Verse 13 is a key verse in Paul's argument. As stated above, Paul sees the works of the flesh as comprising *both* licentiousness *and* legalism. And he is telling the Galatians that they are free from *both*. However, freedom from the Law does not make us lawless. Rather we are led by the Holy Spirit; we are called to a loving relationship rather than a legal requirement. And it is this loving relationship which bears the fruit of righteousness which is manifest in the fruit of the Spirit.

THE WORKS OF THE FLESH

Galatians 5 is well known for Paul's discussion of the fruit of the Spirit. However, before he talks about the fruit of the Spirit he deals with a more distasteful subject: the works of the flesh.

Read Galatians 5:16–21.

How does one avoid fulfilling the lust of the flesh?

What term does Paul use in describing the struggle between the flesh and the Spirit?

What is the result of the work of the flesh?

Below is a list of the works of the flesh from Galatians 5:19–21. Look up these terms in a dictionary and write a brief definition for each.

Adultery

Fornication

Uncleanness

Lewdness

Idolatry

Sorcery

Hatred

Contentions

Jealousies

Outbursts of wrath

Selfish ambitions

Dissensions

Heresies

Envy

Murders

Drunkenness

Revelries

BIBLE EXTRA

Strong's Exhaustive Concordance is a useful tool for investigating the Hebrew or Greek meanings of words in the Bible. Unlike a simple concordance, which only tells you where a word is found, *Strong's* has each usage of every word coded to a numbered dictionary so that you can look up the word in the original language without knowing Hebrew or Greek. Admittedly, the Hebrew and Greek dictionaries included in the concordance give only basic information about the word's origin and meaning, but it is a good starting point. Furthermore, many other resources are available which are coded according to the *Strong's Concordance* numbering.

This is an impressive list, and we can all probably find some work of the flesh which hits uncomfortably close to home. When we recognize that God judges our thoughts and motives, as well as our actions, this list even can become discouraging. Jesus said that adultery is wrong, but lusting after a woman in one's heart is equally wrong (Matt. 5:27, 28). Likewise, murder is forbidden, but anger toward another makes one susceptible to judgment as well (Matt. 5:21, 22). Therefore, everything on this list can be internalized and applied to our inner being as well as our actions.

Paul does not leave us without an answer for the works of the flesh. In the very first verse in this section Paul says, "Walk in the Spirit, and you shall not fulfill the lust of the flesh" (Gal. 5:16). So the solution for our struggle with the flesh is simply to walk in the Spirit. Then we shall not fulfill the lust of the flesh. But how do we walk in the Spirit? And how do we know if we are walking in the Spirit?

OVERCOMING THE FLESH

Read Galatians 5:22—6:10.

List at least three ways to overcome the flesh which are suggested in this passage.

What is the result of living in the flesh? What is the result of living in the Spirit?

Paul says, "If we live in the Spirit, let us also walk in the Spirit" (5:25). What distinctions can you draw between "living" and "walking"?

Paul ends most of his letters with an ethical section, and Galatians is no different. These final segments of his letters provide a lot of practical, hands-on suggestions for living the Christian life. Here Paul gives us several ways of overcoming the flesh.

First, crucify the flesh (5:24). Nobody likes this idea. People are never anxious to die to their own desires—until they hit the bottom. When they finally are reaping the results of the flesh, they realize that those things they embraced brought only corruption (Gal. 6:8). Many people sow to the flesh and then pray for a crop failure! But God has instituted the law of sowing and reaping, and although repentance can cut off some of that harvest, for the most part you will reap in accordance with your works. Therefore, crucify the flesh in order to walk in the Spirit.

Second, accept correction. Galatians 6:1 tells us to restore gently one who has fallen; conversely, we must also accept the correction which others bring. This concept is very important because it shows us again that the church of Jesus Christ is a Body. We are unified with one another, and we need one another. We particularly need this reminder in our American culture because our cultural values tell us to be "rugged individualists." But that is not a value which is grounded in God's Word. Look at the following texts and briefly tell what they say about our being part of the Body of Christ.

1 Corinthians 12:12–26

Philippians 2:1–11

1 John 4:7–21

Third, Paul tells us to examine ourselves (Gal. 6:4). Put in the immediate context, this tells us two things:

1) Examine yourself so that you see a true picture of your-self (6:3), and
2) Examine yourself so that you will not require the correction of others (6:1).

Both of these things require us to be in contact with the Spirit of God and the Word of God, for it is only by the Spirit making use of the mirror of God's Word that we are capable of accurate self-examination.

Finally, Paul tells us not to grow weary (6:9). The law of sowing and reaping applies to good works as well as bad. Yet for some reason it seems that bad works are a lot easier to grow. Anyone who has had a garden knows that it seems to require no work at all to grow weeds. But constant attention is required to grow a desirable plant. Likewise, Paul tells us that we will also reap a good harvest as long as we don't grow weary and lose heart.

LIFE IN THE SPIRIT

In Galatians, Paul has shown that the works of the Law and the flesh cannot perfect our life in Christ. We must walk in the Spirit. This life in the Spirit is a loving relationship which brings freedom rather than bondage. This relationship also bears fruit. We cannot complete a study of this portion of Scripture without examining the fruit of the Spirit. But before we look at the individual qualities which we know as the fruit of the Spirit, we must examine the idea of "fruit."

In my backyard is a pear tree, and this tree is bearing a healthy crop of pears. Throughout this past summer, as I worked in the yard, I never saw the tree working to make pears. I never saw the tree sweat. The tree is producing pears because it has a life-force within it. The pears are a natural expression of the life which is in the tree.

Likewise, we have a new life-force within us. The Holy Spirit indwells us and causes us to produce fruit. We cannot produce the fruit on our own; if we do, it's artificial fruit. It requires the life of the Spirit to bring about the production of fruit.

This does not, however, mean we do nothing. Trees require pruning. Thus, we need to cut off unnatural growth. We all have areas wherein we naturally excel. This is not bad; these things are God-given talents and gifts. Yet it is easy for us to begin to push those areas ahead in our own strength and to neglect areas where God may wish to bring new fruitfulness. So there are times when excess growth caused by our own efforts needs to be pruned back.

Trees also require fertilizer. At the risk of sounding coarse let me say that dead flesh makes good fertilizer. The Bible tells us to crucify the flesh, and it is this very action which will bring an increase in the fruitfulness of our spiritual lives.

Turning now to the fruit itself, get a dictionary and write a short definition for each of the fruits of the Spirit as you did for the works of the flesh.

love

joy

peace

longsuffering

kindness

goodness

faithfulness

gentleness

self-control

 BIBLE EXTRA

One of the basic rules of Bible study is to study biblical concepts in the context of the whole Bible. A dictionary definition is a good way to get a basic idea of a word's meaning, but in the Bible many words take on a particular shade of meaning which can be lost in a simple dictionary definition.

A good method for getting a broader idea of the biblical meaning of a word is to see how the Bible uses the word. For additional study of the fruits of the Spirit, you may wish to find four or five other texts in which each of these words is used and see what ideas are expressed by them.

The growth of the fruit of the Spirit is a process. We need to let that fact be encouraging, not discouraging. If the perfect evidence of the fruit is not fully manifest in your life tomorrow, don't be surprised. If you fail to show evidence of the fruit every time you should, don't be discouraged. Growth is a process.

However, there should be evidence of growth. Are you a little more patient than you were a few years ago? Is your degree of self-control greater than in the past? We need not be discouraged by the gradual nature of growth, but we should be concerned if there is no evidence of growth.

Finally, Jesus said, "As the branch cannot bear fruit of itself, unless it abides in the vine, neither can you unless you abide in Me" (John 15:4). We must remain connected to the life-source if we are to bear fruit, and if we abide in Him, the growth of fruit will surely come to pass.

 FAITH ALIVE

What one "fruit of the Spirit" do you wish to see further developed in your life?

What might be hindering the development of that fruit?

Consider the teaching about that quality you have heard in the past, whether in sermons, lessons, or personal study. How have they helped? What do you need to be reminded of?

Some people have understood Paul to say that the fruit of the Spirit is love, and the remainder of the list is a description of love. Paul also describes love in 1 Corinthians 13. Look at Paul's description and find the common points Paul makes. What is different?

The work of the Spirit is a work of love, and it should produce love in us. As Paul says, "All the law is fulfilled in one word, even this: 'You shall love your neighbor as yourself'" (Gal. 5:14). As we abide in Christ by the work of the Spirit, we experience the freedom from the works of the flesh, and we bear the fruit which no law forbids.

1. *Spirit-Filled Life Bible* (Nashville, TN: Thomas Nelson Publishers, 1991), 1458, "Word Wealth: Matt. 26:41, flesh."

Lesson 6/Faith and the Spirit

One afternoon Paul was sitting at his word processor putting the finishing touches on his letter to the Galatians. Peter, who was visiting from Jerusalem, came in and asked Paul what he was doing.

"I'm just finishing up a letter to the Galatian churches," said Paul. "In fact, I'm glad you're here. In the letter I tell the Galatians about that time a few years ago when I corrected you about withdrawing from the Gentiles. I know it doesn't put you in the most complimentary light, but I think it's related to important points about being free from the Law. You know, that's an important issue in Galatia right now."

"If it will help strengthen the churches, you can certainly tell them that story," responded Peter. "I've goofed enough times that I'm used to having people learn from my mistakes. But besides freedom from the Law, what else are you talking about?"

"Well, I really need to defend my apostleship and the gospel I preach. I know that you, and the other pillars in Jerusalem, have accepted me and my message, but there are still some who insist on attacking the fact that I was not one of the original apostles. Then I talk about freedom from the Law and justification by faith. I have to give them some strong correction on that point, so I want to end with something positive. At the end of the letter I give some encouragement about life in the Spirit. Let me print a copy for you, and you can look it over."

With a few quick keystrokes Paul's old Model II Amanuensis printer came to life and spit out four perfectly printed papyrus sheets. Paul handed the manuscript to Peter and sat down while Peter read the letter.

"Well," said Peter after reading the letter, "as usual you've expressed your ideas in a way that goes far beyond my writing ability. Your emphasis on faith is much needed in Galatia, and probably it will be needed elsewhere at different times."

"Yes," interjected Paul, "I have written with passion and concern, but I hope that others in addition to the Galatians will benefit from this teaching on justification by faith. It is really one of the core issues in the entire gospel!"

Needless to say, that incident did not really take place. However, Galatians has been seen throughout history as one of the great epistles of faith. Galatians, along with Romans, provides more material for the doctrine of salvation by faith than any other part of the Bible, so this reputation and approach to Galatians is well-warranted.

Yet, in our study we have looked at Galatians from a different direction. We have looked at what Galatians has to say about dealing with the kinds of fears we all face. This has been a challenging, yet profitable, course to take in our study, and we have seen the intersection of faith dealing with fear on many occasions. This is not coincidental: faith is the basis for our relationship with God, and we have, time and time again, gone back to the foundation of relationship with God as the foundation for dealing with fears.

As we conclude our study of Galatians we will look more directly at faith as a key topic in Galatians. In addition to faith, we will look at the topics of "gospel" and "Spirit." It is interesting to see how these three topics divide Galatians. The word "gospel" is used twelve times in Galatians, ten of which are in the first two chapters. "Faith" is the term used predominantly in chapters 3 and 4, and more than half the uses of the term "Spirit" are found in chapter 5.

In addition to the distribution of these terms, there is a logical development in Galatians from Paul's defense of his gospel, to the basis or crux of the gospel—which is salvation by faith, to the work of the Spirit which brings new life and empowers us to walk in salvation. So we see that these are topics around which Paul is developing the entire letter. In this concluding study in Galatians we will see how Paul uses these key ideas to develop his teaching and bring unity and coherence to the letter.

GOSPEL

We saw in our first lesson that one of Paul's main purposes in Galatians 1 and 2 is the defense of his apostleship. In addition to this, Paul was also defending his gospel. Paul had gone into Galatia preaching the gospel of grace: salvation comes by faith in Jesus Christ, without works. And he strongly opposed the "different gospel" (Gal. 1:6) to which the Galatians had turned. He goes on to say that this different gospel is not "another" but is a perversion of the gospel.

It is interesting to note that the word "another" used in Galatians 1:7 is the same word Jesus used when He said He would send "another Helper" (John 14:16). Here are some additional insights on the use of that term in John.

 WORD WEALTH

Another, *allos:* One besides, another of the same kind. The word shows similarities but diversities of operation and ministries. Jesus' use of *allos* for sending another Comforter equals "one besides Me. He will do in my absence what I would do if I were physically present with you." The Spirit's coming assures continuity with what Jesus did and taught.[1]

In contrast with John's positive use, Paul is saying, "This different gospel is *not* another. It is not the same type, and it will not bring the same results." In the introduction (Gal. 1:1–10), Paul has some particularly harsh words for those who oppose the gospel and preach "another" gospel.

Read Galatians 1 and 2 and answer these questions about the gospel.

What specific statements does Paul make in defense of his gospel in Galatians 1 and 2?

What does Paul say about different gospels?

What does Paul say about the origin of his gospel?

With whom did Paul communicate his gospel in Jerusalem? Why did he do this and what was their response?

Who did Paul stand against in Jerusalem? Why did Paul take a stand? What was the purpose of those against whom Paul stood?

Look at the following information on the Greek word for "gospel" and answer the questions following.

WORD WEALTH

Gospel, *euangelion:* Compare "evangel," "evangelize," "evangelistic." In ancient Greece *euangelion* designated the reward given for bringing good news. Later it came to mean the good news itself. In the New Testament the word includes both the promise of salvation and its fulfillment by the life, death, resurrection, and ascension of Jesus Christ. *Euangelion* also designates the narratives of Matthew, Mark, Luke, and John.[2]

What allusions does Paul make to the content of the gospel in chapters 1 and 2?

Write a definition of "gospel" based on the above information and Paul's use of the term in Galatians 1:1—2:10.

In defense of his gospel, Paul makes three main points: Paul's gospel
• was not of human origin,
• came through a revelation of Christ, and
• was affirmed by the apostles.

This could be called the historical foundation for confidence in the gospel. (Paul goes on in Galatians to appeal to a scriptural foundation, and an experiential foundation which we will discuss further in the remainder of this lesson.) Paul stresses that the Galatians received the gospel which came directly from the Lord and was in line with the apostolic teaching.

Although it is not Paul's purpose to elaborate the content of the gospel, it was so pervasive in his thought that he could not keep it out of his writing. Paul refers to the Resurrection in Galatians 1:1 and to Christ's substitutionary death in 1:4 and 2:15–21. In addition, we have an example of what Paul taught the Galatians in Acts 13. The crux of Paul's gospel was "Christ crucified, to the Jews a stumbling block and to the Greeks foolishness, but to those who are called, both Jews and Greeks, Christ the power of God and the wisdom of God" (1 Cor. 1:23, 24). The free gift of forgiveness through the death of Jesus was the essence of the gospel, and it is this gospel from which the Galatians are, amazingly, turning.

Throughout the letter Paul expresses his surprise that the Galatians have turned from the gospel (Gal. 1:6; 3:1–3; 4:9). In particular, Paul enunciates a strong distinction between the Galatians having been *called* through the gospel, and those who preach a different gospel being *accursed* (Gal. 1:6, 8). Paul is telling them that they are in danger of walking away from the blessings of grace and moving back under a curse. The words Paul uses for "called" and "accursed" emphasize that he is referring to one's standing with God.

WORD WEALTH

Called, *kaleo:* From the root *kal,* the source of the English words "call" and "clamor." The word is used to invite or summon, and is especially used of God's call to participate in the blessings of the kingdom (Rom. 8:30; 9:24, 25).[3]

Accursed, *anathema:* An animal to be slain as a sacrifice, devoted to destruction. Because of its association with sin, the word has an evil connotation and was synonymous with a curse. In the sacrificial scheme, *anathema* meant alienated from God without hope of redemption.[4]

How do each of these words relate to hope?

Look at Galatians 1:8, 9. Specifically, who is to be accursed if they preach another gospel?

Paul's language shows how serious he is about the message of the gospel. And this is understandable: the gospel is the key to relationship with God, and faith is the key to the gospel.

FAITH

Faith is a key concept in Galatians, as evidenced by the fact that Paul uses the word twenty-two times in the letter. However, Paul begins the letter emphasizing the concept of gospel more than faith; he only uses the word faith once prior to 2:14. The section in which Paul tells of his confrontation with Peter (Gal. 2:11–21) is a transitional section which Paul uses as a springboard to begin his teaching about faith. He then goes on in chapters 3 and 4 to expound his teaching on salvation through faith. He uses both scriptural examples and illustrations to develop his teaching on faith.

Read Galatians 3 and 4.

What are the three main examples or illustrations that Paul uses in these two chapters?

Who is the main Old Testament character Paul uses as an example? Why do you think Paul chose that character?

What idea does Paul use as the diametric opposite to faith?

How do you see Paul showing the relationships among or integrating the concepts of gospel, faith and Law?

In his discussion of faith Paul develops his entire argument on a foundational starting point of faith. His teaching can be outlined as follows:

• The blessing of Abraham comes through faith, but the Law brings a curse.
• Christ has redeemed us from the curse so that we may be blessed.
• The blessing is a promised inheritance.
• The Law was a tutor or master which kept us in bondage until we were to receive the inheritance.
• Christ has brought us into our inheritance, and now we are no longer slaves under the Law.

This entire development is based on the concept of faith, but not just any faith will do. Faith must be in Jesus Christ, who was "clearly portrayed among you as crucified" (Gal. 3:1), and it is the Person and work of Christ which are the grounds of our faith.

SPIRIT

The work of the Spirit is particularly prominent in chapter 5 of Galatians, where Paul is giving instruction concerning walking in the Spirit. Yet there are two other particularly important sections dealing with the work of the Spirit. Read Galatians 3:1–5, and Galatians 4:4–7.

In Galatians 3:2 Paul connects their receiving of the Spirit to their hearing of faith. What does this imply about when the Galatians received the Spirit?

What other statements are made which concern the timing of the Galatians receiving the Holy Spirit?

Paul takes two pairs of ideas which are in contrast to each other. One pair is faith and the Law. What is the other pair of contrasting ideas in 3:1–5, and how do these ideas fit into Paul's overall message?

In our discussion of faith we saw that Paul develops his teaching in five steps. Which one of those steps is the subject of Galatians 4:4–7?

In verse 4 of chapter 4 Paul emphasizes two things about Jesus' coming: He was born of a woman, and He was born under the Law. Why are these two things emphasized?

The first of the above statements, "born of a woman," is translated "made of a woman" in the old King James Version. Does that distinction alter your view of that statement? Why?

These passages bring out some important teaching concerning Jesus and the Holy Spirit. First, it seems apparent that the Galatians received the Spirit when they responded to the word of faith. Within the church of Jesus Christ there are a number of different views concerning the Baptism with the Holy Spirit, the gifts of the Spirit, and speaking with tongues. In spite of many differences, we can be unified in recognizing that salvation is a work of the Spirit. In 1 Corinthians 12:13 Paul says, "For by one Spirit we were all baptized into one body," and the work of the Spirit is to bring liberty and unity. We must learn to recognize our distinctions without allowing them to become walls.

Second, Paul speaks of Jesus "born of a woman, born under the law." This passage is very complex, and much ink has been spilled in elucidating its meaning. The translation of the Greek word *genomenon* poses one problem. The word is literally a form of the verb "to be" and could be translated "becoming." This translation, however, would not make good English. In the first century, it was common for Greek-speaking Jews to use this word meaning "to be born," so that translation is perfectly legitimate.

After determining how the word can be translated, we need to determine what Paul is saying. Some have seen this as a reference to the Virgin Birth, but the terminology used is not so unique as to make that certain. Many scholars agree that Paul is emphasizing Christ's representative role in redemption. Jesus came as One fully human, and as One under the obligations of God's Law. Thus, He fully identified with us and is capable of providing for our redemption.

Finally, Paul's main emphasis on the Spirit is in Galatians 5:16–26. In this passage Paul encourages us to walk in the Spirit. We studied this idea in Lesson 5, but let us again look into this text and glean a few more lessons.

Read Galatians 5:16–26.

What three verbs does Paul use indicating our being guided by the Spirit? What results come out of this guidance by the Spirit?

Compare Paul's statement in 5:17 with Romans 7:13–25. How does the text in Romans help you understand Galatians 5:17, 18?

Paul tells us three ways to function in the Spirit of God. We are to walk in the Spirit (v. 16), be led by the Spirit (v. 18), and live in the Spirit (v. 25).

Walking in the Spirit implies a destination. When we move in the Spirit of God, we find that our resistance to the lusts of the flesh is increased because our focus is on our destination. If one is continually concentrating on what to avoid, he ends up stumbling. But if he concentrates his energy on his goal, then the hindrances seem to fade in importance. Psalm 119:105 says "Your word is a lamp to my feet and a light to my path." In our walk in the Spirit we need God's Word to shine before our feet to keep us from stumbling, and light our path to show us where to go. All the peripheral things can fade into the shadows.

Being led by the Spirit tells us we have a guide. As we move toward our destination we need One who can help us choose the right path for our circumstance. When the gold hunters went to California in 1849 they all did not go the same way. A good guide would consider the size of the company, the type of equipment available, and the amount and type of livestock when he chose a path. During the journey the guide might have to make changes because of unexpected weather conditions or enemies on the path. Likewise, we need the guidance of the Holy Spirit to give us specific, personal direction as we pursue God's calling for our lives.

Finally, living in the Spirit implies purpose. Paul connects the concept of living in the Spirit to two things: walking in the Spirit, and living with one another (Gal. 5:25, 26). We do have a destination and a guide. And in a very real sense our entire lives are the journey to this destination, so living in the Spirit is a walk in the Spirit. In addition to that we have a purpose during the journey. We are responsible for one another, and our relationships will have a great impact on our own development. As Proverbs says, "As iron sharpens iron, so a man sharpens the countenance of his friend" (Prov. 27:17). Living in the Spirit involves the purpose of helping others to develop, and in fulfilling that purpose, we always find that we, too, are strengthened.

 ### FAITH ALIVE

The message of Galatians is a message of freedom: we are free from the Law and free from sin. We have grown from being children under a tutor to being full heirs. Now we need to walk in that freedom, which means walking in the Spirit, being led by the Spirit, and living in the Spirit.

How have you been led by the Spirit?

How has the leading of the Spirit affected your walk in the Spirit?

How has it affected your relationships with others?

As we close Galatians, let us remain mindful of Paul's exhortation:

"Stand fast therefore in the liberty by which Christ has made us free, and do not be entangled again with a yoke of bondage." (Gal. 5:1.)

1. *Spirit-Filled Life Bible* (Nashville, TN: Thomas Nelson Publishers, 1991), 1603, "Word Wealth: John 14:16, another."

2. Ibid., 1468, "Word Wealth: Mark 1:1, gospel."

3. Ibid., 1773, "Word Wealth: Gal. 1:6, called."

4. Ibid., 1736, "Word Wealth: 1 Cor. 12:3, accursed."

Lesson 7/The Beginning of the Thessalonian Church

If you were to visit Thessalonica today you would find a large, modern city. The factories of the city churn out their daily quota of steel, chemicals, textiles, and pharmaceuticals. Trains, boats, planes and trucks in continuous movement form a web of transportation with Thessalonica at the center. The city is the second largest in Greece, and boasts a history as rich and diverse as any in the world.

Almost two thousand years ago, Paul visited Thessalonica, and he found it much the same. Although it did not have airplanes and chemical factories, Thessalonica was a major commercial and transportation center in the first century. Paul may have thought this city would be the location for him to fulfill the Macedonian call (Acts 16:9–10), but he was forced out of the city after a short stay. Thus, he had to build the fledgling church of Thessalonica by means of correspondence rather than in person.

Paul's two epistles to the Thessalonians give us a great deal of insight into the attitudes and feelings of the people involved. These letters were written during times of great trial and success. His work in Thessalonica was a microcosm of these times in both his success and his trials, and the keys to his success and his endurance are seen in these letters. These keys are the foundations upon which we will focus our study of Thessalonians. But we will begin by examining the circumstances in which the gospel first came to the Thessalonians.

THE HISTORICAL RECORD

We are told of the beginning of the Thessalonian church in Acts 17. Paul had come from Philippi where he had been "spitefully treated" (1 Thess. 2:2) and made a two-day journey to Thessalonica. He apparently left Luke in Philippi to help establish the fledgling church there and traveled on with Silas and Timothy. We will begin our study of Thessalonians by examining the record of Acts, but first let us look at some background on the city itself.

 BEHIND THE SCENES

Thessalonica was a significant city; in fact, it was the capital of the senatorial province of Macedonia when Paul and his group arrived in A.D. 50 or 51. The city lay at the intersection of the Via Egnatia, which was the major highway running across the Balkan peninsula, and the main road from the Aegean to the Danube. Paul had taken the Via Egnatia from the time he crossed from Troas into Europe, and he may have intended to cross the Balkan Peninsula and go on to Italy when the events in Thessalonica diverted him.

Unlike Philippi, Thessalonica had a large Jewish community, attested to by the fact that there was a synagogue. This, along with the strategic situation of the city on a major highway to Rome, and the importance of the city itself, led Paul to preach in Thessalonica.

Read Acts 17:1–15 and Acts 18:1–11.
How successful was Paul's preaching in Thessalonica?

Who believed Paul's message?

How long was Paul in Thessalonica?

What events compelled Paul to leave?

Where did Paul go after leaving Thessalonica? Who went with him?

What happened in Berea?

Where did Paul go next, and who went with him?

Where did Silas and Timothy rejoin Paul?

Is there a conflict between 1 Thessalonians 3:1, 2 and the record of Acts? If so, how can it be resolved?

When Paul arrived at Thessalonica, he preached in the synagogue, as was his custom, and he had success among some of the Jews as well as many of the God-fearing Greeks. Some of the prominent women were also converted (Acts 17:4).

Acts tells us that Paul reasoned with the Jews for three Sabbaths. After that, some of the Jews gathered some agitators (humorously designated a "Rentamob" by F. F. Bruce[1]) and caused an uproar in the city. The mob did not find Paul, but they dragged Jason, his host, to the city rulers and accused him of harboring people who were fomenting sedition. The rulers took security from Jason, which probably indicated that Jason took responsibility for the behavior of the missionary band.

Acts tells us that the believers sent the missionary band away that very night. The group left the Via Egnatia and traveled south to Berea. They may have thought they would have less trouble off the main road, but it was not to be. Jews from Thessalonica came to Berea and caused trouble there as well. So Paul went on to Athens, leaving Silas and Timothy in Berea.

During Paul's stay in Athens, Timothy joined him. But Paul was concerned about the Thessalonian church with whom he had so little time. So Paul sent Timothy back to Thessalonica to check on the progress of the believers. Paul then went on to Corinth.

While in Corinth, Silas and Timothy rejoined Paul. They had a good report from Thessalonica, and Paul was greatly encouraged. Paul wrote his first letter to the church in Thessalonica, encouraging them and correcting some errors which had crept into the teaching. Later during that same stay in Corinth, Paul also wrote Second Thessalonians.

Paul speaks a great deal of the Thessalonians' reception of the gospel in his letters to them. Thus, we have much specific information about the attitudes and actions of the apostles in bringing the Word, and the Thessalonians in receiving it.

HOW THE GOSPEL CAME TO THE THESSALONIANS

In examining the coming of the gospel to Thessalonica, we have a key verse to guide us:

"For our gospel did not come to you in word only, but also in power and in the Holy Spirit and in much assurance, as you know what kind of men we were among you for your sake." (1 Thess. 1:5)

Paul elaborates this idea more fully in chapter two, and his references to the behavior of the apostles fit the three points he gives in the above verse. We will examine chapter 2 of 1 Thessalonians to find examples of the missionaries' behavior which illustrate these points, but first let us look more closely at the first descriptor: power.

        WORD WEALTH

Power, *dunamis:* One of four great power words. The others are *exousia,* delegated authority; *ischuros,* great strength (especially physical); and *kratos,* dominion, authority. *Dunamis* means energy, power, might, great force, great ability, strength. It is sometimes used to describe the powers of the world to come at work upon the Earth and divine power overcoming all resistance. (Compare "dynamic," "dynamite," and "dynamometer.") The *dunamis* in Jesus resulted in dramatic transformations. This is the norm for the Spirit-filled and Spirit-led church.[2]

Read 1 Thessalonians 2:1–12 and categorize Paul's statements about the apostles' behavior into the three categories given in 1 Thessalonians 1:5.

The apostles came:

1. In power = _____

2. In the Holy Spirit = _____

3. In much assurance = _____

Paul states that the gospel came, not only in word, but in power. The record in Acts does not tell of any specific miracles which occurred in Thessalonica. Rather, Luke focuses on Paul's debating and persuading the Jews in the synagogue that Jesus was the Christ. However, there are two reasons that we can be sure that there were great works which occurred during Paul's ministry in Thessalonica. First, the normative experience of the early church was to see signs and wonders, both as signs to the multitudes and as provision of wholeness for people. Second, in the verse cited above, Paul strongly implied that great works were done to which the Thessalonians were witness.

Another evidence of the power in which the apostles came was the boldness with which they spoke. The word Paul used when he said "we were bold in our God to speak to you the gospel of God in much conflict" (1 Thess. 2:2) is the verb form of "boldness" described below.

WORD WEALTH

Boldness, *parrhesia:* Outspokenness, unreserved utterance, freedom of speech, with frankness, candor, cheerful courage, and the opposite of cowardice, timidity, or fear. Here it denotes the divine enablement that comes to ordinary and unprofessional people exhibiting spiritual power and authority. It also refers to a clear presentation of the gospel without being ambiguous or unintelligible. *Parrhesia* is not a human quality but a result of being filled with the Holy Spirit.[3]

Paul came to the Thessalonians with power and boldness. In both these words we see that the Spirit of God was the enabler. Paul did not minister out of his natural talents, even though his natural talents were immense. Rather, he depended on the Holy Spirit to energize and direct his work, which brings us to his second point: the gospel came "in the Holy Spirit."

We are told in 1 Thessalonians 2:3 that the teaching of the apostles did not come from error. Also, verses 3–5 tell us that the apostles did not come with deceit, man-pleasing, flattery, or covetousness. In other words, the apostles came with truth and integrity. This is no surprise, for the Holy Spirit is the Spirit of Truth (John 16:13). Just as we saw that the Holy Spirit was the power behind the boldness of the apostles, likewise He is the source of truth and the One who motivated us, as He motivated the apostles, to be people of integrity.

Finally, the apostles came "in much assurance." In speaking of this aspect of their ministry, Paul uses the tender and intimate illustration of a nursing mother's love for her children (1 Thess. 2:7). He speaks in particular of the gentleness and generosity of the apostles as they work among the Thessalonians.

This too is a work of the Holy Spirit. The Holy Spirit is seen in Scripture as a dove: gentle and innocent. And the fruit the Spirit produces—love, patience, kindness, goodness—is reflective of His nature. It is, therefore, no surprise that these characteristics are modeled by the messengers of the Spirit.

HOW THE THESSALONIANS RECEIVED THE GOSPEL

The Thessalonians also had their part in receiving the gospel. As we saw in Acts, Paul and his band were in Thessalonica for less than a month before trouble was stirred up which drove them from the city. The Thessalonian letters indicated that the persecution did not end with the departure of the apostles.

Read 1 Thessalonians 2:13–16 and 2 Thessalonians 1:1–5.

What specific statements indicated that the Thessalonians were undergoing persecution?

Who were the persecutors?

With whom does Paul compare the Thessalonians? Why?

Why does Paul say the Judeans are "contrary to all men"? What does he mean by that statement?

What does Paul mean by the phrase "wrath has come upon them to the uttermost"?

PROBING THE DEPTHS

Anti-Semitism?

This passage in Thessalonians contains some of Paul's harshest words against his countrymen. Throughout church history there have been those who, unfortunately, isolated words like these from the totality of Paul's teaching and found occasion herein for anti-Semitic activity. But to understand the meaning of these verses, we first need to see the overall framework of biblical teaching within which this passage occurs.

First, we must understand that the Bible teaches that all are sinners, and it was the sin of each and every one of us that put Jesus on the cross. No single race or group can be blamed for the Crucifixion of Jesus Christ.

Second, we need to understand Paul's perspective. Paul made a number of very harsh statements against the Jews in his writings; he also made some of the most hopeful statements for the Jews. Paul had a deep love for his countrymen, as evidenced by Romans 9:3 where he says he could wish himself accursed for their salvation. Yet he also dealt with the frustration of the continual opposition of some Jewish Christians as well as those opponents who remained Jewish.

Thus, in seeking to understand passages like this one in Thessalonians, we must recognize that Paul is speaking primarily of his opponents. He is certainly not saying that all Jews are contrary to all men; he himself was a Jew—and proud of it. His condemnation was for those who opposed the message of the gospel and kept people from the saving knowledge of Christ Jesus.

Paul's statement about wrath coming upon them is variously interpreted. The difficulty lies in the fact that the past tense is used which seems to indicate that the wrath spoken of either has happened or is in progress. Some commentators say this is referring to final judgment, and Paul uses the past tense (Greek-aorist tense) to stress the completeness of the judgment.

Other commentators suggest that Paul is referring to an event or series of events that had recently occurred which were an expression of God's wrath. Two events occurred in A.D. 49 which fit into this interpretation. First, Claudius Caesar expelled the Jews from Rome; second, there was a massacre in the Temple courts during the Passover. If Paul were alluding to one or both of these events, the past tense, of course, is natural.

The Thessalonian church had begun amid persecution, and it was continuing to grow amid persecution. The key to this steadfastness in the face of persecution is stated in 1 Thessalonians 1:6:

> "And you became followers of us and of the Lord, having received the word in much affliction, with joy of the Holy Spirit."

We see in Acts and Thessalonians that the church was born and grew amid continuing persecution. Five to six years later Paul speaks to the Corinthians about the trial the Macedonian churches are still facing (2 Cor. 8:1, 2). Yet this trial was successfully faced because they received the Word, not only with affliction, but also with joy in the Holy Spirit.

Look again at 1 Thessalonians 2:13–16 and 2 Thessalonians 1:1–5 and list references which show the fruit of the Spirit in the lives of the Thessalonians. (The fruit of the Spirit are found in Galatians 5:22, 23.)

Therefore, just as we saw that the Holy Spirit was active in the work of the apostles and in their presentation of the gospel, likewise the Holy Spirit was at work on the receiving end. The Holy Spirit brought the Thessalonians to Christ, but the Thessalonians also had examples to follow. In fact, the Thessalonians both followed examples and became examples themselves.

Read 1 Thessalonians 1:6–10; 2:13–16.

The Thessalonians could be called followers of three groups or persons. List them.

1.

2.

3.

To whom were the Thessalonians examples?

Of what were the Thessalonians examples?

The Thessalonians became examples of true repentance. Even in the midst of persecution they followed the Lord and supported one another. They continue to be an example even today, for they show us that:

• in whatever we are facing we can look to those who have faithfully walked through the same things before us,
• we can face trials successfully in the joy of the Holy Spirit, and
• we can endure tribulations by letting love abound one to another and allowing the mutual support of the whole body to aid us in our weakness.

 FAITH ALIVE

In this lesson we have seen that the Holy Spirit was the enabler for the apostles to present the gospel and for the Thessalonians to receive the gospel. Likewise, we need to continue working on the Holy Spirit in us to enable us.
In what area of your life do you need to allow the Holy Spirit to enable you to succeed?

What is a trial you are personally facing?

How does the example of the Thessalonians help you in facing your own trials?

1. F. F. Bruce, *Word Biblical Commentary*, Volume 45, 1 & 2 Thessalonians (Waco, Texas: Word Books, Publisher, 1982), p. xxiii.

2. *Spirit-Filled Life Bible* (Nashville, TN: Thomas Nelson Publishers, 1991), 1632, "Word Wealth: Acts 4:33, power."

3. Ibid., 1632, "Word Wealth: Acts 4:31, boldness."

Lesson 8/The Work of Faith— Foundations for Freedom I

What do you think of when you think of freedom?

In our materialistic, hedonistic society many people think that winning the lottery would give them real freedom. They would be free from the need to work. They would be set for life and could do whatever they wanted to do.

"Doing whatever you want to do" is a key component of our society's concept of freedom. Look at the popular mottos of today's world:

Just do it.

If it feels good, do it.

You only live once.

I did it my way.

From every direction, we are bombarded with messages which tell us that our individual fulfillment is the goal of life, and freedom is being able to heap upon ourselves whatever pleasure we think will fulfill us without having to struggle to obtain it.

Yet it was not always so.

In the past freedom was seen as the ability to make responsible choices. It was being able to choose significant elements of life without external coercion or compulsion. One was free to weigh the costs and risks of his or her choice and to pursue it to the extent that his or her resources and abilities allowed.

The Pilgrims chose to come to the New World so they could worship God in the way they chose. They deemed the risks worth the benefit, and many did not live to see the realization of their dream. Yet they were free in their choice.

The Founding Fathers literally risked "our lives, our fortunes and our sacred honor" to fight for an ideal: the idea that a government could be established within which people could freely make choices in religion, expression of conscience, where and how they would live, and with whom they would associate.

In these cases we see that our forebears did not have a shallow conception of freedom, nor did they believe that freedom was without cost. Our modern idea of freedom as automatic and without cost or boundaries is an aberration.

It is important that we confront our society's conception of freedom as we begin a study of the foundations of freedom in Christ, because our freedom in Christ is not the shallow, irresponsible freedom that the world peddles. Freedom in Christ is the freedom to make responsible choices, with a clear assessment of the consequences and responsibilities which go along with the choices.

Thus, as we study these foundations of freedom, we will see that these are not foundations which have been laid down, once and for all, for our benefit; rather, they are foundations which we each need to lay in our own lives, in order that a solid and true freedom can be built.

The first foundation stone for freedom in Christ is the work of faith. This may sound like an odd term because we usually contrast works and faith. However, works and faith are in opposition to one another only when one tries to work for his own salvation. Paul speaks of a work *of* faith which grows out of our faith in Christ and helps us to become like Him. In Thessalonians we see three aspects of this work of faith.

RECEIVE THE WORD

We have seen how the Thessalonian church began. The gospel gained a beachhead in Thessalonica in spite of many obstacles, and a key to the success of the gospel in Thessalonica was how they received the Word. Receiving the Word is a key to the work of faith, and the Thessalonians can teach us valuable lessons.

Read 1 Thessalonians 2:13—3:13.

List two or three characteristics of how the Thessalonians received the word.

Paul says he wanted to visit the Thessalonians, but Satan hindered him (1 Thess. 2:18). How do you think Satan hindered Paul?

Why did Paul send Timothy to Thessalonica?

Explain Paul's statement in 3:8.

The Thessalonians received the gospel as Scripture, in suffering, and steadfastly.

First, chapter 2 verse 13 tells us the Thessalonians correctly discerned the gospel to be the Word of God and not just the word of man. An evidence and a result of their reception of the Word was the effective working of the Word within them. Let's look at that word *effectively*.

WORD WEALTH

Effectively, *energeo:* One of the four big energy words: *energeo, energes, energia,* and *energema.* The words all stem from *en,* "in," and *ergon,* "work," and have to do with the active operation or working of power and its effectual results.[1]

Paul is saying that God's Word is powerful, it contains transforming power which will work in those who are open to receive its impact. This concept is not peculiar to Paul. See also Hebrews 4:12; Isaiah 55:11; and Psalm 107:20.

Second, as we have seen, the Thessalonians received the Word in suffering. Paul makes an interesting statement in regard to their suffering. He says, "you yourselves know that we are appointed to this" (1 Thess. 3:3). The idea of suffering for the gospel is not popular in the church today, yet the Bible teaches us that we will suffer.

There are three ways in which we suffer. First, all people suffer as a result of being fallen human beings living in a fallen world. Job said, "Man who is born of woman is of few days and full of trouble" (Job 14:1). And Paul reminds us that all creation was subjected to the bondage of corruption (Rom. 8:19–21). So we, along with all mankind, will experience certain troubles as a result of the fallen condition of the world.

But we will suffer also as Christians. Jesus said, "If they persecuted Me, they will also persecute you" (John 15:20). We have all faced ridicule or mocking because we stand for Christ. Some of us have faced the loss of relationships. A few have even faced physical harm because of their walk with Jesus. Regardless of the apparent degree of suffering, we have seen and we have shared in suffering for His sake.

Finally, we suffer in a manner which overlaps with the others and thus is not always recognized. Paul says here that we are appointed to suffer. In Colossians he makes an even more dramatic statement:

"I now rejoice in my sufferings for you, and fill up in my flesh what is lacking in the afflictions of Christ, for the sake of His body, which is the church" (Col. 1:24).

Paul is saying there is a sense in which he himself, and the church, will suffer in order to complete (fill up) the sufferings of Christ. Now we must be very clear about what this concept does **not** mean. Paul is not saying there is any sense in which we must suffer to pay for our own sins or the sins of any other. Christ alone is our Redeemer, He alone died once for all, and His work on the Cross is the sole basis, and the complete, adequate and sufficient sacrifice for our sin. However, in some manner it has pleased God to allow the church to participate in suffering as part of the outworking of His plan. How this suffering accomplishes God's will is one of those things which we "see through a glass darkly," but, like Paul, we can rejoice in our sufferings knowing that God's will and work are being done.

 BIBLE EXTRA

There are many passages in which Paul speaks of his suffering and the suffering of the people of God. To put together a more complete picture of Paul's thought on this subject you may wish to examine the following passages:
Romans 8:17
2 Corinthians 1:5–7
2 Corinthians 4:7–18
Philippians 1:27–30
2 Timothy 2:10
Additionally, a good commentary on Colossians will provide further explanation and background on Colossians 1:24. Two commentaries which will give a fuller explanation of that verse are the *Word Biblical Commentary,* Volume 44, Colossians and Philemon; and the *Tyndale New Testament Commentary,* Volume 12, Colossians and Philemon.

Finally, the Thessalonians received the Word steadfastly. Paul speaks openly of his anxiety for the Thessalonians and of his relief to find them standing fast. His statement in 3:8 seems to be saying, "Life is not worth living if my work comes to naught." But even beyond that, Paul seemed to put a special emphasis on their steadfastness. This may be explained by looking again at that time in Paul's life.

We know that Paul had received a dream calling him to come into Macedonia (Acts 16:9, 10). Yet when he went into Macedonia, he faced one problem after another. He was imprisoned in Philippi, he was run out of Thessalonica, and then those who ran him out of Thessalonica followed him to Berea. In Athens he did not successfully start a church, and he went to Corinth "in weakness, in fear, and in much trembling" (1 Cor. 2:3). Paul was probably wondering if he had really heard God's call.

But the report of Timothy of the steadfastness of the Thessalonians put his fears to rest. God *had* raised up a church, and they were growing even in the midst of trials. God *had* called him, and his work would remain. Paul could endure the suffering if he knew that it was for the cause of Christ and it was furthering His cause.

Read 1 Thessalonians 3:11–13.

In this prayer Paul again mentions his desire to visit the church. Yet beyond that he is praying that the receiving of the Word will bear its fruit.

Paul prays for three specific things. List them.

1.

2.

3.

Which of these things can be seen as the outgrowth of their reception of the Word?

Verse 13 begins with "so that." This indicates that verse 13 is dependent upon, or built on, what precedes it. How is the request in verse 13 connected to verse 12?

Receiving the Word is the first step in the work of faith, and it bears the fruit of love and holiness. Yet we must note that again Paul tells us that our walk with the Lord is not a private affair. We need to grow *with* one another in love so that we can be established in holiness. We also need those who are examples, which brings us to the next element of the work of faith.

FOLLOW THE FOLLOWERS

In Thessalonians, as in other writings of Paul, we see that Paul is not afraid to be an example. He knew that he was following Christ, thus he was able to tell people to follow him.

Read 1 Thessalonians 2:1–12.

List four or five adjectives telling how the apostles proclaimed the gospel.

In what way was the apostles' ministry "motherly"?

In what was their ministry "fatherly"?

How did the apostles support their ministry? Why?

Verse 6 says they might have made demands as apostles. What kind of demands could they have made?

What statements are made which illustrate the apostles' integrity?

The apostles here are shown to be shining examples of forthright, honest, loving behavior. Look at the characteristics which they modeled in proclaiming the gospel. The apostles were:
- Bold in proclaiming the gospel (v. 2)
- Correct in proclaiming the gospel (v. 3)
- Honest in proclaiming the gospel (v. 3)
- God-pleasing in proclaiming the gospel (v. 4)
- Not greedy in proclaiming the gospel (v. 5)
- Humble in proclaiming the gospel (v. 6)
- Gentle in proclaiming the gospel (v. 7)
- Loving in proclaiming the gospel (v. 8)
- Giving in proclaiming the gospel (v. 9)
- Devout in proclaiming the gospel (v. 10)
- Just in proclaiming the gospel (v. 10)
- Blameless in proclaiming the gospel (v. 10)
- Instructive in proclaiming the gospel (v. 11)
- Comforting in proclaiming the gospel (v. 11)

The scope of this study does not permit a thorough treatment of each one of those qualities, but we can focus on three. First, the apostles were correct in proclaiming the gospel. We need to ensure that our grounding in the Word is accurate. The study of the Bible and doctrine ought to be an important part of our lives because *what* one believes *is* important. It is true that God looks on the heart, not the mind. But it is also true that salvation does not come by hearing about Jesus and thinking He was a great teacher. What we believe matters. Therefore, the correctness with which the apostles proclaimed the gospel is an important guide for us. We, too, need to strive for correctness in our own proclamation of the gospel and in our own beliefs.

That being so, we also need to be humble. Authority in doctrine can make one into an intolerant, pompous Pharisee unless it is mixed with humility. Along with a sincere striving for correct doctrine, we must humbly recognize that we are servants—not lords. We ought to serve one another (John 13:13–17), and we ought not judge another's servant (Rom. 14:4).

Finally, we must be loving. The essence of the fruit of the Spirit is love, and love should permeate all that we do. The development of any of these qualities requires the work of the Spirit: He is the Spirit of Truth, and He guides us to correctness in teaching. He is the Dove; He comes with humility and teaches us to be like Him. But the most basic characteristic of the Spirit's work is love. His work flows out of love, for love is a basic attribute of God.

BEAR UP IN AFFLICTIONS

The final part of the work of faith is bearing up in afflictions. We have seen how the Thessalonians received the gospel with suffering, but here we want to focus on endurance.

Read 2 Thessalonians 1:1–12.
Why does Paul give thanks for the Thessalonians?

What are Paul's reasons for boasting?

What does Paul say is evidence of the righteous judgment of God? How does this illustrate the righteous judgment of God?

What requests is Paul praying for in verse 11?

What is the calling Paul refers to?

In this passage Paul speaks of the patient endurance of the Thessalonians. Their endurance in affliction provides a manifestation of God's righteous judgment, for it shows that God is righteous in His final judgment of persecutors. For if the believers endure persecution without retribution, then it is just that the retribution fall upon the persecutors at the judgment, and that those who are troubled now have rest and peace.

But beyond that, the endurance of the Thessalonians in faith and love provides a witness of their calling. As Paul says in verse 11, our calling is to fulfill God's good pleasure and the work of faith.

These two aspects of our calling ultimately merge into one. From God's side, He is calling *us* to fulfill His good pleasure, yet it is also He who works *in us* to will and do His pleasure (Phil. 2:13). From our side, we do the work of faith, yet ultimately our source is God, for it is His power in us which energizes us for the work of faith.

FAITH ALIVE

The apostles are to be examples to us. Those characteristics which describe how they proclaimed the gospel should be qualities which are growing in our own lives as well.

In which of those qualities do you particularly feel you need growth?

In which area has the Lord been working with you lately?

How is the example of the apostles a comfort or an encouragement to you?

1. *Spirit-Filled Life Bible*, (Nashville, TN: Thomas Nelson Publishers, 1991), 1827, "Word Wealth: 1 Thess. 2:13, effectively."

Lesson 9/The Labor of Love— Foundations for Freedom II

Tony was smitten by Cupid's arrow, he had fallen head over heels in love, he was enamored, he was twitterpated. So he wrote to his beloved the following letter expressing his heartfelt devotion:

My Dear,
    You are the sunlight to me. My every thought is filled with thee. I would do anything to be with you. I would climb the highest mountains, swim the swiftest rivers, and cross the widest deserts to be at your side.

                                    Your Beloved Tony

P.S. I'll see you Saturday . . . if it doesn't rain.

This little story shows us two things. First of all, it is funny because of the magnitude of the gap between Tony's romantic language and his true devotion. Second, the opening description shows us that we have many ways to speak of infatuation or romantic love—but are we able to describe what real love is?

If there is a concept about which our society is more confused than the concept of freedom, it is probably the concept of love. However, the direction in which our society has warped both concepts is the same. In both cases we have moved the idea from something of great value, something which makes demands, and something to be diligently guarded, to something cheap, irresponsible, and easy.

Love is marvelously complex. Love is caring. Love is giving. It is wishing for the best for another and doing all one can to provide the best. It is sometimes inciting another to strive for the best when he or she is willing to settle for less. Love requires one's entire being. It is spiritual, and intellectual, and emotional, and physical. Love is enduring and longsuffering; it continues even when faced with rejection.

But the marvelously complex thing about love is that none of those qualities makes love by itself, yet the lack of any of those qualities destroys love. Love is a holistic concept: one cannot analyze the pieces and know love; it must be found as a whole.

And love, like freedom, requires work. Along with their work of faith, Paul commended the Thessalonians for their labor of love. Their love for one another and for the Lord had been tested in the crucible of persecution and been purified. But that is not to say it had been perfected. Paul has words of correction and exhortation as well as words of commendation and encouragement as he addresses the Thessalonians' labor of love. And from his instruction to the Thessalonians, we can learn about the freedom that is built on the labor of love.

Love Abounds

Paul was greatly encouraged by Timothy's report of the Thessalonians' faith and love (3:6). Yet Paul was not about to let his young church rest on its laurels. In the brief section of the letter between 3:12 and 4:12 Paul prays that their love may increase and abound, and he goes on to exhort them twice to let their love abound and increase more and more. Paul was intent on seeing love abound so that the fruit of love would come to maturity.

Read 1 Thessalonians 3:11–13.

The form of this passage is that of
A. an exhortation
B. a prayer
C. a blessing
D. teaching

Who is the source of the love?

Who is to be the recipient of the love?

What is the result of the love?

Who establishes their hearts in holiness?

Is His action dependent on our love? Why?

A key result of the labor of love is that we are established in holiness. Let's look more closely at the word "holiness" in order to understand what Paul is saying here about the labor of love.

 WORD WEALTH

Holiness, *hagiosune:* The process, quality, and condition of a holy disposition and the quality of holiness in personal conduct. It is the principle that separates the believer from the world. *Hagiosune* consecrates us to God's service both in soul and in body, finding fulfillment in moral dedication and a life committed to purity. It causes every component of our character to stand God's inspection and meet His approval.[1]

A central idea in the concept of holiness is separation from the world, and it is here that we see the intersection of the labor of love and being established in holiness: our labor of love separates us from the world by giving us a goal, or focal point, outside the world, and our labor of love manifests to the world that we are separate. Jesus said that the world would know we are disciples because of our love for one another (John 13:35). Furthermore, He said the world would hate us (John 15:18). So, we get the picture of the believers loving one another, that manifestation of love showing the world that we belong to Jesus, and oddly, the world hating us because of it. So we see that the old saw about everyone loving a lover is not true.

Why should the world hate the lovers?

The world hates us because we are not of the world, and our love is not of the world. The genuine, God-given love manifested in us will show up the world's love as inadequate, hollow. The world at its best can reveal a facsimile of perfect love, as Paul says in Romans, "Perhaps for a good man someone would even dare to die" (Rom. 5:7). But perfect love is usually not heroic in that spectacular sense. It is, day in and day out, consistent; it is there even when inconvenient, and even in unglamorous circumstances. The love which we are to manifest as disciples surpasses what the world can produce.

It also surpasses what we can produce. We cannot find this kind of love within ourselves, and we cannot generate it. We need to allow the Lord to make us "increase and abound in love" even as this passage says.

Verse 12, where that statement is made, is particularly interesting because it can be interpreted in two ways. First, one could say that the source of love is the Lord, and He makes us abound in love by infusing us with more love. Second, one could say that we are the source of love, and the Lord instigates or induces the growth of that love.

How do we determine which shade of meaning is more adequate? The best way to answer a question like this is to allow the Bible to comment on itself. The Bible is its own best commentary, and we can gain a clearer perspective on this question by examining what else the Bible says about love.

Read 1 John 4:7–21.

List the reasons why we ought to love one another.

How is God's love manifest toward us according to this text?

How do we know that we know God?

In this passage John indicates in several ways that God is the source of love. In fact, in many New Testament manuscripts verse 19 says, "We love because He first loved us." This is not to say that God never incites us to love, but that ultimately the source of all love is God.

Another important aspect of love which John makes very clear is that love involves others. One cannot isolate himself and claim to have been perfected in love. As we consider the labor of love in 1 Thessalonians, we will see that Paul also strongly identifies the labor of love with our conduct toward one another.

Love Is Pure

Read 1 Thessalonians 4:1–8.
What is the theme of this section?

In what does Paul want them to abound?

What commandments were given by the apostles?

To what is Paul referring with the phrase "his own vessel"?

How are we to possess our own vessels? How is this done?

Rewrite verse 6 in your own words.

Note the words "sanctification" and "holiness." What does this passage tell us about those qualities?

Paul gives very direct and specific instructions in this section regarding sexual purity. In the culture of Greece and Rome this was necessary instruction. Although the Greeks and Romans practiced monogamy, it was more a legal construction than a practical reality. Having mistresses or affairs was common and accepted. Indeed, in the second century Tertullian remarked, "We Christians hold everything in common except our wives. You Romans hold nothing in common except your wives."

Moral purity was in short supply in the Roman Empire, so direct, practical instruction in morality was necessary. In fact, part of the training of catechumens in the early church was the study of Proverbs. This study was done specifically to develop a foundation in moral character. Interestingly enough, one of the appeals of Judaism (and later, Christianity) was its high moral standards. Many people were seeking a moral foundation in the midst of that quicksand of amorality.

Therefore, when Paul forthrightly addressed the issues of sexual conduct, he did so because it was a very real problem in that society, not because he was some kind of prude who wanted to make sure nobody had fun.

    PROBING THE DEPTHS

1 Thessalonians 4:4
Paul uses a figurative expression when he says that each should "possess his own vessel in sanctification and honor." The meaning of this phrase is complicated by the use of the word "vessel." There are two basic interpretations.

The first, and more popular of the two, is that vessel refers to the body. Within the context of the passage this makes sense and is a natural reading. The weakness of this interpretation is that the word translated "possess" is normally translated "acquire," and it is absurd to think of Paul telling someone to acquire a body. However, the grammatical construction here permits the translation "gain control over" or "possess."

The other possible translation is that "vessel" refers to one's wife. According to this translation Paul is saying that each should acquire his own wife (see 1 Cor. 7:2). This translation retains a more natural reading of "acquire," but does so at the expense of providing a more unnatural reading of "vessel."

Another possibility is that "vessel" refers to wife, yet Paul is not just saying that each one should acquire his own wife. Rather, Paul is making a statement about relationships within marriage. Paul could be saying that a couple's intimate relationships should be honorable and sanctified, not driven by lust as the Gentiles. By this interpretation Paul says that intimate relations within marriage should not just be an animalistic, hormonal drive to physiological ecstacy. Rather, Paul is saying that a couple's intimate relationships can be, and should be, sanctified and honorable without being any less fulfilling.

LOVE IS COMMUNAL

Read 1 Thessalonians 4:9–12.

List two reasons Paul gives for not needing to write them concerning brotherly love.

Why, then, does Paul exhort them about brotherly love?

What three directives does Paul give concerning walking properly toward those outside?

What is the other reason Paul gives them the three directives noted above?

Paul uses two distinct words for love in verse 9. Examine the following definitions and answer the questions below.

 WORD WEALTH

Brotherly love, *philadelphia:* From *phileo,* "to love," and *adelphos,* "brother." The word denotes the love of brothers, fraternal affection. In the New Testament it describes the love Christians have for other Christians.[2]

Loved, *agapao:* Unconditional love, love by choice and by an act of the will. The word denotes unconquerable benevolence and undefeatable goodwill. *Agapao* will never seek anything but the highest good for fellow mankind. *Agapao* (the verb) and *agape* (the noun) are the words for God's unconditional love. It does not need chemistry, an affinity, or a feeling. *Agapao* is a word that exclusively belongs to the Christian community. It is virtually unknown to writers outside the New Testament.[3]

Is Paul making a distinction by the use of these two words in verse 9? Why do you think so?

The only other time Paul uses the word *philadelphia* is in Romans 12:10. Does that reference alter your view of what Paul is saying? Why?

Paul's use of the term "brotherly love" probably was not meant to be set in contrast to "love" later in verse 9. Paul's use of the term in Romans is positive, so we know that he used the term in reference to a quality which Christians should exhibit.

Throughout this lesson we have repeatedly seen the communal, or corporate, nature of love expressed. We saw that Jesus said our discipleship was manifest in our love for one another. Our examination of 1 John 4 revealed God as the source of love, but again stated that this love was shown in relationship. Paul exhorted the Thessalonians about the proper and improper expressions of this love among the brethren. And here again we see this emphasis on the corporate aspect of love.

But here again, Paul is very practical. Our love is to be expressed in concern and care for one another, but we also need to mind our own business. This is a balance which requires wisdom, and, in this passage, Paul gives us little to guide us to that balance. But he provides three directives: to live quietly, to mind our own business, and to have a business to mind. How do these statements help us find that fine line between being a brother and being a busybody?

Paul's first statement is translated, "aspire to lead a quiet life." This statement is actually an oxymoron. The word translated "aspire" means "strive for" or "work hard for." So Paul is saying, "Work hard for stillness," or "Strive to not strive." Paul probably uses this device to get the attention of the listeners. But he is saying also that the quiet, peaceful life does not come naturally; we have to work for it. His next two statements tell the Thessalonians how to work for it. Mind your own business and have a business to mind. These certainly are not an all-inclusive list of directions for leading a quiet life, but it apparently was what the Thessalonians needed.

In summary, Paul was telling the Thessalonians that their love had to be a balanced mixture of concern and leaving alone. The key to knowing how to achieve that balance is also the key to loving. As we have seen, God is the source of love. He is love's origin, and He is the essence. He is also the One we can ask for wisdom. "If any of you lacks wisdom, let him ask of God, who gives to all liberally and without reproach, and it will be given to him" (James 1:5). As we have seen throughout our lessons, the answers continually come back to our relationship with God. This is truly the foundation for everything in our lives.

    FAITH ALIVE

We began this lesson by speaking of love as a rich mixture of qualities, the absence of which destroys love. In Thessalonians we have seen a few of these qualities in greater detail. We ought to see these qualities in our own lives, yet none of us have these qualities perfected.

What qualities or characteristics of love do you understand better as a result of this lesson?

What qualities of love have you seen which require more development in your own life?

We all need Paul's exhortation to "increase more and more" in love (1 Thess. 4:10). To do so we must remember that God is the ultimate source of all love, for without Him, we can do nothing (John 15:5).

1. *Spirit-Filled Life Bible* (Nashville, TN: Thomas Nelson Publishers, 1991), 1829, "Word Wealth, 1 Thess. 3:13, holiness."
2. Ibid., 1889, "Word Wealth, Heb. 13:1, brotherly love."
3. Ibid., 1578, "Word Wealth, John 3:16, loved."

Lesson 10/The Patience of Hope— Foundations for Freedom III

Jim was making his usual commute to work through the Southern California traffic. Suddenly a car passed him quickly on the right, swerved in front of him, and continued into the left-hand lane. As the car passed in front of him, Jim noticed the bumper sticker: "In case of Rapture, this car will be driverless!" Jim smiled wryly. *That might be an improvement,* he thought.

Whether it is tritely expressed on a bumper sticker or seriously and thoughtfully expounded in the study of prophecy, the Second Coming of Christ is the blessed hope of believers. The Thessalonian epistles contain some of Paul's most extensive teaching about the end times, and his teaching about the Rapture and the "son of perdition" are included with many other texts as people attempt to determine a chronology of the last days.

As interesting and valuable as these studies are, they do not focus on the primary message that God is giving us in these prophecies. The main point of prophecy is not prediction—but hope. We have a hope which the world does not have, for our hope is a real, enduring, eternal hope for the future.

The world, on the other hand, has no lasting hope. The world may see a brighter future, but it is always a temporary utopia. We may envision a better world, but it is always haunted by the failures of the past. Even when, beyond hope, the best possible turn of events has occurred, the problems and difficulties of the future hover like a shadow on the horizon. The world has no lasting hope, and the world knows it. It is expressed in songs like "Dust In the Wind," or this excerpt from "The Story In Your Eyes":

> Listen to the tide slowly turning
> Wash all our heartaches away.
> We're part of the fire that is burning,
> And from the ashes we can build another day.
>
> But I'm frightened for your children
> That the laughter we are living is in vain,
> And the sunshine we've been waiting for
> Will turn to rain.[1]

This view of the future may seem overly pessimistic, but it is actually very honest and logical. We cannot control events so as to produce and maintain anything positive for very long. If there is no God—and the world believes there isn't—then an honest assessment of our past and present leaves no hope for the future.

In strong contrast to that, the Bible gives us reason to hope. First, we do have a God who is bigger than the failings of mankind. Second, our God not only knows the future, He also holds the future. And we have the promise of Christ's return, which is not just a fire escape; it is the hope of seeing God's reign established on earth.

It is of this hope that Paul is speaking in Thessalonians. And he calls the Thessalonians to patient endurance in holding on to that hope. It is a hope that calls us to patience in the present by focusing on the future, for our patience in hope is based on the Blessed Hope.

THE BLESSED HOPE

The Second Coming of Christ has always been called the blessed hope of believers. That name comes from Titus 2:13 where Paul tells Titus to teach his congregation to live soberly, "looking for the blessed hope and glorious appearing of our great God and Savior Jesus Christ." That hope was always a key element of Paul's teaching. In Thessalonians, among Paul's earliest letters, teaching about the Second Coming figures prominently. In Titus, one of Paul's last letters, he is still exhorting that the blessed hope be a key part of the church's teaching.

To understand the idea of a blessed hope we need to see what kind of hope Paul is talking about. People use the word "hope" in many different ways. People "hope for a better world," and they have a warm, fuzzy feeling about "things being better sometime." But this hope is ephemeral; it is not based on anything more than wishful thinking. People hope to win the lottery, but they know that the odds are fourteen million-to-one against it. In contrast to these hopes, Paul speaks of a hope that is solid and sure.

     WORD WEALTH

Hope, *elpis:* Hope, not in the sense of an optimistic outlook or wishful thinking without any foundation, but in the sense of confident expectation based on solid certainty. Biblical hope rests on God's promises, particularly those pertaining to Christ's return. So certain is the future of the redeemed that the New Testament sometimes speaks of future events in the past tense, as though they were already accomplished. Hope is never inferior to faith, but is an extension of faith. Faith is the present possession of grace; hope is confidence in grace's future accomplishment.[2]

The following texts do not all refer to the Second Coming, but they all illustrate that steadfast hope. Looking at these texts and their contexts, describe how the hope spoken of illustrates the definition above. Describe how the hope is connected to the blessed hope.

Romans 15:4

2 Corinthians 1:7

Colossians 1:5

Hebrews 6:18, 19

In addition to our hope being steadfast and grounded, Paul says we have a *blessed* hope. Let us see what implications are found in the word Paul uses to describe our hope.

WORD WEALTH

Blessed, *makarios:* From the root *mak,* indicating large or of long duration. The word is an adjective suggesting happy, supremely blessed, a condition in which congratulations are in order. It is a grace word that expresses the special joys and satisfaction granted the person who experiences salvation.[3]

This definition suggests at least three things. First, this hope is our great hope. It is a hope which is a foundation to other hopes. Second, this hope is our happy hope. This hope makes us joyful; we are looking forward to our hope with glad expectation. Third, this hope is founded in grace. We do not deserve the blessing of this hope, nor can we earn it. But our hope is based on the work of Christ; thus it is a certainty because Christ's work is completed (Heb. 10:11–13).

Read 1 Thessalonians 4:13—5:11 and answer the following questions.

What is the main subject of 1 Thessalonians 4:13–18?

What does Paul mean by his reference to "those who have fallen asleep"?

Upon what belief does Paul base his confidence that the dead will be raised?

When will the dead in Christ be raised?

What is the theme of 1 Thessalonians 5:1–11?

How does Paul describe the "day of the Lord"? Is this description applicable to believers or nonbelievers?

How are we described as believers?

Since we are "of the day," what kind of conduct should we exhibit? Why?

What does Paul say about our behavior toward one another?

During Paul's short time in Thessalonica the Second Coming of Christ had been a key component of his teaching. We know this because of the issues he deals with in the Thessalonian correspondence. In 1 Thessalonians Paul has to discuss what happens to believers who die before the Second Coming. The very fact that this question came up indicates that the early church expected the return of the Lord to be soon. Paul assures them that those who "sleep" (an idiomatic expression for death) would be raised at the coming of the Lord and would meet the Lord with us. This was to be a source of hope for the believer: not only do we have the hope of the Lord's return, but we also have the hope of the joy of being reunited with those we love.

Paul also speaks of the "catching away" of the believers at the Second Coming of Christ. This event is usually called the Rapture. The term "rapture" is not used in the Bible, but here, and elsewhere, the idea is expressed clearly enough to be assured of its truth. Paul uses the words "caught up," which indicate a rapid, energetic event.

WORD WEALTH

Caught up, *harpadzo:* To seize, snatch away, catch up, take by force. The word describes the Holy Spirit's action in transferring Philip from one location to another (Acts 8:39) and Paul being caught up to Paradise (2 Cor. 12:2, 4). It suggests the exercise of sudden force.[4]

So we see that the return of the Lord was an earnest expectation of believers. This hope was the answer to their concerns and a guide to their conduct. Paul continues in chapter 5 with a discussion of how this hope affects their actions.

Unlike the unbeliever, who is not aware of the signs of the times, the believer walks in the light. As children of the light we are to live in the light. This entails a state of mind (soberness), a state of readiness (put on the armor), and a hope (appointment to salvation). These three conditions are integrated in our lives and affect our behavior. Being sober, we do not live or participate in the dissipation of the way of the world. Yet that does not make us somber or grim; as ones who have hope, we are truly the most joyful people on earth. Being called to readiness, we do not share the same priorities as the world. Our priorities reflect our desire to serve the One who called us. This does not mean we have no participation with the world, but it does imply that there will always be some friction between us and the world, for we are not going in the same direction.

Read 2 Thessalonians 1:6–12.
What event is Paul talking about in verses 7 and 8?

Is Paul speaking of the same event in verses 9 and 10? Why?

How do the event(s) here fit together with the Rapture?

What is the calling of which Paul speaks in verse 11?

How does this passage relate to the patience of hope?

Paul is actually speaking again of the Thessalonians' work of faith, and he is urging them to be steadfast in the midst of tribulation. However, as we saw in the definition of hope, faith and hope are connected. They are each a different perspective on the accomplishment of grace. Faith stands in present possession of the working of grace while hope looks forward to the future possession of that work of grace which is yet to be fully accomplished.

As we have seen, the work of grace yet to be accomplished includes Christ's return and our reuniting with the believers who have gone on before us. Here in 2 Thessalonians we also see that God's judgment is a work of grace in a sense. To us who are saved, it is the final sealing of the grace we received at the Cross. But to the unbeliever the Judgment will not be a work of grace, but a work of justice—they will truly get what they deserve.

 BIBLE EXTRA

The events of the end times which are spoken of in 1 and 2 Thessalonians can be correlated with each other in several different ways. Add to these the other texts throughout Scripture which deal with last things, and one has a study which goes well beyond the scope of these present lessons.

There is no shortage of books on prophecy, so further resources are readily available. But to do a thorough study of prophecy one must be aware that there are many different views. A balanced study will examine and seek to understand differing views of the end times. The Spirit-Filled Life Study Guide titled *Focusing on the Future* will provide an introduction to differing views on prophecy and provide an understanding of concepts which are foundational to a study of prophecy.

HOPE UNSHAKEN

As we have seen, the Second Coming of Christ was a key part of Paul's teaching to the Thessalonians, and he firmly establishes the fact that our hope is based on this blessed hope. Yet the Thessalonians found this hope shaken, and Paul had to deal with these doubts and questions.

Look again at 1 Thessalonians 4:13–18.

Why did Paul write this passage?

What questions had arisen in the minds of the Thessalonians that Paul is addressing?

Read Thessalonians 2:1–12.

Why does Paul write this passage?

What issue had shaken the Thessalonians?

Why had that question come up?

What is "that Day"?

What two things does Paul say will precede "that Day"?

Who is the lawless one?

What distinction can be made between the "mystery of lawlessness" and the "lawless one"?

What is the destiny of the lawless one?

Why will God send a strong delusion?

It is interesting to note that Paul wrote both of these well-known prophetic passages in answer to questions or errors which were creeping into the church's teaching. These texts tell about the end times, but that is secondary to the apostle's purpose. Paul's primary purpose is to ensure that the Thessalonians have a firm grasp on the hope that sustains us.

In 1 Thessalonians Paul was answering a question about believers who died prior to the Lord's return. His express purpose is that we do not sorrow "as others who have no hope" (1 Thess. 4:13). In Paul's mind establishing the distinction of "we who have hope" as opposed to "others who have no hope" was the primary purpose of this teaching about the Second Coming; detailing a chronology was secondary—if it was in his mind at all.

Likewise, in the passage from 2 Thessalonians Paul wrote to correct error and maintain the clarity of our hope in the minds of the believers. Apparently an erroneous teaching had come into the Thessalonian church; from whence, we are not told. However, someone was teaching that the day of Christ had already passed (2 Thess. 2:2). Paul does not specifically state the origin of the error, but he mentions three sources of error: "by spirit or by word or by letter, as if from us" (2 Thess. 2:2). These three sources of error bear looking into because the same sources of error are active today.

The gifts of the Spirit are gracious expressions of the work of the Lord among us, but we must use wisdom in the application of the gifts and in judging them. It is possible that the confusion among the Thessalonians had come about because someone had "prophesied" that the day of Christ had passed. Erroneous prophecy did occur in the early church; Paul had to address a case in Corinth (1 Cor. 12:1–3), and he tells the Corinthians to judge the prophecies (1 Cor. 14:29). Likewise, we need to use wisdom in discerning what messages are truly from the Lord, and we have three sources upon which to draw. First, the Holy Spirit will say nothing which contradicts the eternal Word. The Bible is our first source of judgment. Second, we have pastors and elders who are mature in the Lord and can give counsel in discerning whether or not a message truly originates from the Spirit. Finally, the same Holy Spirit dwells in us. If He is giving a message to the church or to you personally, He can bear witness to it in your own spirit.

The second way this error may have arisen was "by word." False teaching was alive in the church from the beginning, and it is still alive today. To combat false teaching, we must know the Bible—it is the foundation of our doctrine. However, we must also interpret the Bible rightly. An important factor in proper interpretation that has been long overlooked in Protestant circles is interpreting the Word within a body of believers. We need the Body of Christ to help balance our interpretation of the Word. I believe much of liberal Protestant theology would not have originated if the theologians had not been separated from the rank and file of the Body and left to do theology in a sterile academic setting. We need to have the balance provided by relationship with the Body because our life in Christ is a relationship, not merely an intellectual exercise.

Finally, error can come from "letter[s], as if from us." This is related to the previous point, but I want to focus on false teachers rather than false teaching. Today there are many who claim to be spiritual teachers. These teachers claim to have some source of authority which gives them the privilege to advise others on the proper way of life or the way to God. Once again our best defense is to be grounded in the Truth, and the way to be grounded in Truth is to be in the Word and the Body. Reading the Bible and regular fellowship with other believers will go a long way toward maintaining your walk with God.

THE RESULTS OF HOPE

Finally, our stand on the blessed hope has definite results. In addition to the desired result of maintaining our readiness, our hope provides results which are internal—which affect our spirits. Look at 1 Thessalonians 4:13—5:11 and note the results of this hope.

What are the results of our hope which are alluded to in this passage?

How are we to help one another in light of our hope?

What are the results of our hope according to 2 Thessalonians 1:5–12?

How do these results relate to each other?

The hope of the Lord's coming involves the hope of our joy to see Him, and the hope of our joy to be united with the whole Body of Christ. The loved ones we have known, and brothers and sisters we have not known, will be reunited in the biggest family reunion of all time. In addition to this, we will see the Lord who loved us and gave Himself for us.

The results of this hope are threefold. First, we do not sorrow. We have assurance that we will be reunited with those we love. Because of that our grief over the temporary separation at death is not like the grieving of the world. Our loss is only for a little while.

Second, we can comfort and edify one another. Our basis of hope allows us to encourage each other with the reminder of this hope. And our hope is a foundation which can be built upon; our edification is founded on the hope that we are building for a purpose which lasts well beyond this life on earth.

Finally, as we walk in this hope, the Lord Jesus Christ is glorified in us. This steadfast hope makes us different from the world. Unlike the fleeting or groundless hope of the world which we described in the introduction to this lesson, our hope is firm and our future is assured. Thus our walk in this hope becomes both a witness and a means of glorifying our Lord. We have hope for the future because our hope is in the One who holds the future.

 FAITH ALIVE

Look up the following verses and see what additional information they tell us about our hope.

Romans 5:1–5

Ephesians 4:4

Colossians 1:27

We have repeatedly emphasized that our hope is sure and steadfast, but our foundation for freedom requires *patience* in hope. However, this patience is not a grueling endurance test. We have the comfort and edification of our brothers and sisters in Christ. Together we look forward in joy to the hope of the coming of our Lord Jesus Christ and all that includes.

1. Justin Hayward, *"The Story In Your Eyes," Legend of a Band* (New York: PolyGram Records, Inc., 1989).
2. *Spirit-Filled Life Bible* (Nashville, TN: Thomas Nelson Publishers, 1991), 1826, "Word Wealth, 1 Thess. 1:3, hope."
3. Ibid., 1410, "Word Wealth, Matt. 5:3, blessed."
4. Ibid., 1830, "Word Wealth, 1 Thess. 4:17, caught up."

Lesson 11/Your Election By God— Foundations for Freedom IV

The day has finally arrived! The National Football League draft is here! All the teams have their initial picks laid out, the press is anxiously waiting, agents and players await breathlessly. Who will be the first pick?

Being chosen first inevitably means fame and fortune. A big contract and commercial endorsements are the spoils of the contest. The Heisman Trophy winner is there with his agent. The Butkus Award winner is watching anxiously on television. The All-Americans wait to hear if they will get an offer.

Now the moment has come. The first team steps to the microphone to announce the very first pick of this year's draft! They have selected . . . Leo Loadstone?

There is a moment of stunned silence. Who on earth is Leo Loadstone? Then the press starts scrambling, trying to find out about this new star. Where did he go to school? Where does he live? Why was he chosen? Why hasn't anyone heard of him?

When Leo is finally found it is discovered that he was the quarterback of a junior college intramural flag football team which came in last in its division. The news is shocking and questions abound. Rumors fly that organized crime is somehow involved, or the team owner has had a mental breakdown.

Finally, the owner has a press conference to clear up the questions. He steps up to the bank of microphones and bluntly states his convictions. "I have the team that I need to win the Super Bowl, and to prove that I already had what it takes to win it all, I chose Leo to lead the team to the Super Bowl. I could have chosen anyone, but he was my choice. And I am giving him the team and the resources necessary to win the big one."

This may sound like an impossible dream, but it has happened in a venue far more important than the NFL. We have been chosen, and God's choice was not determined by anything we had which made us a worthy choice.

In our discussions of foundations for freedom we have looked at several things which involve our work. This is not to say that we are buying or earning freedom, but rather the walk of freedom involves actions which we participate in.

In this lesson we will look at the final foundation for freedom which, in a sense, is the basis for the rest: our election by God. This aspect of our foundation for freedom, unlike the others, is entirely the work of God. We do not participate in His choosing us, we do nothing to be chosen, and we do nothing to deserve being chosen. God's election is wholly a matter of grace.

Our election by God is generally thought of in reference to salvation. But either our concept of election is too narrow, or our concept of salvation is. Our election by God has implications which go far beyond the gift of forgiveness—as great as that is. Our election has consequences which go beyond a point in time when we came to the saving knowledge of Jesus Christ. It relates to our entire life and walk in the Spirit, and to our growth in the truth.

CHOSEN FOR SALVATION

The key verse for studying this topic in the Thessalonian epistles is 2 Thessalonians 2:13:

> "But we are bound to give thanks to God always for you, brethren beloved by the Lord, because God from the beginning chose you for salvation through sanctification by the Spirit and belief in the truth."

This verse must be carefully studied to ensure that we understand what Paul is saying. Paul is obviously saying that we are chosen for salvation, but we need to determine how the ideas of "salvation," "sanctification," "by the Spirit," "belief," and "in the truth" all relate to one another.

What does the phrase "by the Spirit" describe?

What does the phrase "in the truth" describe?

How do the two phrases above relate to the root idea of "salvation"?

What are we saved *through*?

The manner in which I formerly understood this verse was that God chose us for salvation through sanctification, and He chose us through the Spirit and because of our belief in the truth. Another way one could understand the relationship of these ideas would be that God chose us for salvation, which comes through sanctification and which comes through the Spirit. However, both of these understandings are wrong.

This verse tells us that God chose us for salvation. Salvation comes, or is affected in our lives, in two ways: first, through sanctification by the Spirit, second, by belief in the truth. Having now understood the relationship between these terms, let us look more closely at the meanings of the terms.

WORD WEALTH

Salvation, *sotera:* Compare "soteriology." Deliverance, preservation, soundness, prosperity, happiness, rescue, general well-being. The word is used both in a material, temporal sense and in a spiritual, eternal sense. The New Testament especially uses the word for spiritual well-being. Salvation is a present possession (Luke 1:77; 2 Cor. 1:6; 7:10) with a fuller realization in the future (Rom. 13:11; 1 Thess. 5:8, 9).[1]

Here we see that salvation is far broader than forgiveness. The forgiveness of our sin is the initiation of salvation, but it is only the beginning of the blessings of salvation. Salvation includes the ongoing working of wholeness in one's spirit, soul, and body. As such, it is a continuing process as well as a completed work. The completed portion of the work is our standing in Christ: we are totally forgiven and justified in Him. The process is the work of the Spirit *making* us more like Christ.

This process is sometimes called sanctification, yet that usage is only partially correct. Let us examine the verb form, "sanctified," to get a grasp on this word.

WORD WEALTH

Sanctified, *hagiadzo:* Compare "hagiography" and "Hagiographa." To hallow, set apart, dedicate, consecrate, separate, sanctify, make holy. *Hagiadzo* as a state of holiness is opposite of *koinon,* common or unclean. In the Old Testament things, places, and ceremonies were named *hagiadzo.* In the New Testament the word describes a manifestation of life produced by the indwelling Holy Spirit.[2]

In the New Testament there are passages which speak of our sanctification as an accomplished fact (1 Cor. 1:2; Heb.

10:10). There are other passages which speak of a process of sanctification (John 17:17–19; 2 Tim. 2:21). So we see that sanctification, like salvation, is a process which is accomplished in one sense, yet it is also ongoing and not yet completely realized.

This ongoing process is a work of the Spirit in one's life, thus we see that the entire Trinity is involved in the work of our salvation. The Father has chosen us. The work of Jesus Christ is the means of salvation, and the ongoing process of sanctification is the work of the Holy Spirit. Our election by God means that one of the great works of God is going on in *us!*

The Scripture tells us of other works wherein the Trinity is involved, and these works are always great works in God's plan. In creation we see the work of the Trinity as God spoke and brought creation into existence by the power of the Word. The Spirit of God brooded over the waters (Gen. 1:1, 2; John 1:1–3; Col. 1:16). In the Incarnation the Holy Spirit came upon Mary and the power of the Highest overshadowed her as Christ was incarnated within her (Luke 1:35).

Here in Thessalonians the Trinity is again at work, and *you* are that work! You are a new creation in Christ Jesus. Jesus has come into you, and He is growing within you. And this holy work which is ongoing in your life is not your work; it is not by your effort, and it is not because you did anything to deserve it. It is because **God chose YOU!**

This is why the foundation of election by God is the basis for all the others. It is because we have confidence in God and His work that we can look forward in hope to the completion of His work at the day of Jesus Christ. Because God has chosen us we have a reason to work in faith and love: we know His work will be accomplished, so we know that our work also has a purpose. In fact, this element of our working together with God is shown in the final statement Paul makes in 2 Thessalonians 2:13: We are chosen for salvation through belief in the truth.

There are two things we must note about our belief in the truth. First, this statement in verse 13 needs to be understood as a direct contrast to those "who did not believe the truth" in verse 12. Those who do not believe the truth are condemned, while we who believe the truth experience salvation. Second, lest we think our election is our choice, we must recall that "by grace you have been saved through faith, and that not of yourselves; it is the gift of God" (Eph. 2:8).

The words translated "belief" in 2 Thessalonians 2:13 and "faith" in Ephesians 2:8 are the same word. So both of these verses are speaking of our salvation by means of believing (or faith in) the gospel. Yet both of these verses also make it clear that the source of salvation lies wholly in God. We are saved by His grace, and we are saved by faith which is His gift. In this study we cannot delve into the many questions regarding the roles of God and the believer in choosing to be saved. But we must see that this text is emphasizing God's side of the work because God's work forms the foundation for all that we do.

COOPERATION WITH GOD

Having established these key ideas in Paul's discussion of election by God, we may now see what else he tells the Thessalonians about election. Read 2 Thessalonians 2:13–17.

To what did God call the Thessalonians (verse 14)? For what purpose was this call made?

What are the Thessalonians commanded to do?

To what epistle does verse 15 refer?

What is the work of Christ in verses 16 and 17?

How do verses 16 and 17 relate to what Paul said earlier?

God chose and called the Thessalonians unto salvation. And as we have already seen, this salvation begins with redemption, but goes far beyond that into every area of our lives. This salvation makes demands upon us as well. This foundation of election calls for us to establish those other foundations we have been discussing. As Paul says in verse 15, our stand in the truth is founded on the call of God.

In verses 16 and 17 we again see Paul turning to consider the action initiated by God. It is God who has given us consolation and hope, and it is Christ who establishes us. In our consideration of this topic of election we see Paul constantly turning back and forth between God's activity and our activity. This is because, with this concept of election, we are broaching a great mystery which has been the cause of years of theological debate: to what extent do we choose God and to what extent does He choose us? The Bible teaches that both choices are involved, but how they relate or interact is beyond the wisdom of man to discern.

In this study we have focused on the fact of God's election and what that means *for* us rather than dwelling on the questions which surround the topic. And we see that we are chosen for salvation, yet salvation is a process as well as an event. In this process we cooperate with God's work. Look at 1 Thessalonians 5:1–8.

What are we called in this passage?

How did we achieve that title?

In light of these facts, how should we act?

What specific contrasts in behavior does Paul appeal to?

It is because we are chosen that we have come into the light and are now sons of the light. Our own works did not achieve that position for us; it was God's call which brought us "out of darkness into His marvelous light" (1 Pet. 2:9). As sons of the light, we are called to a different lifestyle. Rather than slothfulness and drunkenness, we are called to be watchful and sober. This all belongs to our cooperation with God, and it is all for a purpose.

APPOINTED TO SALVATION—SAVED FROM WRATH

Read 1 Thessalonians 5:8–11.
Why do we behave as sons of the light?

To what does the wrath of God refer?

What is the basis of our salvation?

How are we to treat one another? Why?

On the face of it, behaving as children of the light in order to avoid the wrath of God may seem an unworthy response to God's love. However, we need to see that verse 9 is better seen as a purpose than a result. God does not keep us out of His wrath because we behave correctly—that is slipping back into the concept of salvation by works. Rather, God has appointed us to salvation and not to wrath; therefore, we respond in love and gratitude.

But even that modification does not give us the full picture. We also need to keep going back to the broader concept of salvation which we discussed earlier. This salvation is grounded in Christ's work as verse 10 says. But the ongoing process of salvation calls us and requires us to live like children of the day. So we see that we behave as we do, not to avoid wrath, or even in gratitude for salvation. But we behave as we do *because* we are children of the light—we are children of the Father of lights. His light and His salvation are working in us, and if it is working in us, it will eventually work its way out and be manifest in our lives.

 FAITH ALIVE

Our election by God needs to be understood against the background of a broad view of all that salvation means. How has your perspective on salvation been expanded by this study?

In addition to seeing a broader view of salvation, we have also seen that the Trinity is working in each of us to accomplish that salvation. With this in mind, comment on Philippians 1:6.

Our election by God is a great truth. Elements of it may be shrouded in mystery, but what has been revealed causes us to glory in our salvation and say with Paul,

"Oh, the depth of the riches both of the wisdom and knowledge of God! How unsearchable are His judgments and His ways past finding out! 'For who has known the mind of the Lord? Or who has become His counselor? Or who has first given to Him and it shall be repaid to him?' For of Him and through Him and to Him are all things, to whom be glory forever. Amen." (Rom. 11:33–36).

1. *Spirit-Filled Life Bible* (Nashville, TN: Thomas Nelson Publishers, 1991), 1553, "Word Wealth: Luke 19:9, salvation."

2. Ibid., 1594, "Word Wealth: John 10:36, sanctified."

Lesson 12/Lifestyles of the Freed and Fearless

Freshly showered and shaved, Larry donned his letterman's jacket, into which he could just fit after twenty-five years. He was preparing to go to his high school homecoming football game. Over the years he had been to a number of homecoming games, but this year was going to be special. Twenty-five years earlier the team on which he had played won the state championship. Now, they were having a special team reunion. In addition, the football coach, who had led their team to the title and continued a solid, winning tradition, had just announced his intention to retire after thirty-four years of coaching. The school had prepared a special half-time show honoring its state champions from twenty-five years earlier, and had planned a post-game reception for the team and the coach.

The night was unseasonably warm for early November, but a jacket was still necessary. The home team was in excellent form, and routed the visitors 35–7 to the delight of the partisan crowd. The half-time show was well received, as team members and alumni relived the glory of that championship season. Larry thought the night was perfect.

The post-game reception was no less an extravaganza. Members of the press were there, the mayor was present, even the state senator was on hand to honor the coach. But the highlight of the night came when the coach spoke.

"Ladies and Gentleman, I have had the honor of being the focal point of this evening, and the greater honor of coaching a lot of fine boys for the past thirty-four years. Throughout those years I have had many good teams, and a few great teams, but my most memorable team is, of course, the team that won the state title. Winning a championship like that is something most coaches never get. I had that privilege once, and those memories will be with me the rest of my life.

"But let me tell you something: that championship team was not the best team I ever had. They had their share of talent—I remember in particular the offensive line, anchored by the Hoffstater twins. But I had other teams which had more size, more speed, and more skill. The championship team of 1970 was great because of their relationships. Those boys knew that they needed each other, and—if I may say so—they knew they needed me. I never had a group which, as a whole, listened to me better. I never had a group which supported one another more."

"Many people have been tempted to make football a picture of life. It isn't. Football is a game, and no game can be an adequate picture of the complexity and struggle of life. What football can do is teach boys to relate to one another and support one another—in good times and in bad, in monotonous practice drills and in game-breaking plays. If through my work I have taught some boys that they cannot be men by themselves, then the past thirty-four years have had results which reach far beyond a dusty trophy case."

As he drove home, Larry pondered those words, "they cannot be men by themselves." Coach had said it better than he had ever thought. The biggest lesson he learned as a member of that championship team was that he needed others. That lesson had served him well through college, in marriage, and in business. After twenty-five years he was still learning from the coach.

Throughout our studies in Galatians and Thessalonians we have also seen that our growth and victory come through relationships. We have seen that the work of the Spirit and life in the Spirit is an integral part of living in liberty. Above all, we have seen again and again that our relationship with God is the basis of all the answers.

However, we have also seen that life in the Spirit includes life in the Body of Christ. We need one another. Just as the coach pointed out that Larry's team was great because they depended on and supported one another, likewise, we need one another to reach the goals which God has for us. We, too, cannot be people of God by ourselves.

God has ordained that our walk in the Spirit also be in the Body. So as we consider the lifestyle we pursue in freedom, we must look again at the full range of relationships: our relationships with all people, our relationships with believers, and our relationship with God.

AN OTHER-DIRECTED LIFESTYLE

Life in the Spirit always involves others. There is no way to get around the fact that God intended us to be relational people. Furthermore, our relationship is not intended to be only with God. We need relationships with others as well. Read 1 Thessalonians 5:12–15 and see what directives Paul gives concerning relating to others.

Paul tells us how we ought to relate to different groups or categories of people. What is the first category of people concerning which Paul gives us directives?

What commands are we given concerning this group?

What other groups of people does Paul mention?

What specific directions are given concerning particular categories of people? Why does Paul give those specific commands?

From Paul's specific directions can you deduce a general principle?

What commands does Paul give us which apply to our relationships with all people?

Compare 1 Thessalonians 5:15 with Matthew 7:12. How are they similar? How are they different?

Here at the end of 1 Thessalonians, Paul tells us how we should treat various groups of people. He begins by telling us how we ought to treat our pastors, elders, and others who labor for the Body of Christ. The directives are simple and straightforward: recognize them and esteem them very highly. The main lesson we can derive from this text relates to the expression "esteem them very highly." The word which is translated "very highly" is related to the word translated "abundantly" in John 10:10. Look at the meaning below.

 WORD WEALTH

Abundantly, *perissos:* Superabundance, excessive, overflowing, surplus, over and above, more than enough, profuse, extraordinary, above the ordinary, more than sufficient.[1]

This definition tells us that our esteem and respect for our leaders definitely should be something above the ordinary. However, the word Paul uses in 1 Thessalonians has the prefix *hyper* before it. This indicates that we ought to go beyond even what was described above. It is as if Paul is saying we should esteem them with extra-superabundance.

Do we show that kind of esteem to church leaders? Not often. We have a very human tendency to be critical. It is much easier to be critical than it is to honor, and our leaders, being human, have their own failings which become all the more apparent because they are in the public eye. However, Scripture tells us to honor them, and esteem them very highly. We must strive to achieve that balance of honoring our leaders for the ministry they have been given while still recognizing that they too are brothers and sisters who need our love and support and correction.

Paul gives further direction in 2 Thessalonians regarding how to treat leaders. In this case the leaders are he and the others who had established the church in Thessalonica, but the request given certainly applies to all leaders.

Read 2 Thessalonians 3:1–5.

For what specific things does Paul request prayer?

For what does Paul pray for the Thessalonians?

What does this text tell you concerning your own leaders?

Pray for your church leaders. We are directed to pray for them so that the gospel may spread, and they will be protected from "unreasonable and wicked men." Frequently, we can end up in the position of "unreasonable," for we tend to put super-human expectations on leaders. A good attitude toward our leaders will be much easier to maintain if we pray for them more and criticize them less.

In addition to leaders, Paul gives specific directions concerning the unruly, the fainthearted, and the weak. In each of these cases Paul gives a specific direction which deals with the situation involved. Is someone unruly or insubordinate? They get warned. We are not told precisely what they are warned about, but one can assume that they are warned to straighten up or face discipline.

The fainthearted were to be comforted. We frequently have little patience with the fainthearted. With something less than love we tell them that life is rough; they had better learn to deal with it. But does that show the love of Christ? No, "a bruised reed He will not break, and a smoking flax He will not quench" (Is. 42:3). Likewise, we need to be examples of Christ in comforting the fainthearted.

Finally, we uphold the weak. In our society the strong survive, but in the Body of Christ "none of us lives to himself, and no one dies to himself" (Rom. 14:7). We are told to uphold the weak, for we are all one.

Each of these cases has several basic principles in common. First, these directives are frequently counter to what the world would do. Second, each situation is met with an appropriate response. That is, the way we respond to particular issues must fit the issue involved. Finally, and most importantly, it requires wisdom to achieve a proper response. In these responses, Paul shows insight and wisdom. Thankfully, we have the same Source of wisdom to guide us.

Paul gives three exhortations which apply to everyone: be at peace, be patient, and pursue what is good. There is a subtle difference in the first two commands. We are to be at peace among ourselves; this applies primarily to the relationship of believers to one another. But Paul says to be patient with all. This distinction relates to the fact that peace implies a harmony and oneness which is appropriate to believers with one another but foreign to the relationships of believers and unbelievers. On the other hand, patience is a key characteristic of love (1 Cor. 13:4) and is to be shown to all.

Verse 15 might be called the corollary to the Golden Rule. If we are to do as we would that others do to us, then it logically follows that we do not pursue retribution, but Paul goes beyond that. This statement actually takes the Golden Rule to its highest level of interpretation. Not only are we to treat people as we wish to be treated, but we actively seek the best for all people at all times.

So we see that Paul is direct and practical in his insistence that our lives be directed outward to others. Yet, as we saw in our study of the labor of love, he also demands orderliness so that the witness of the church not be hindered.

AN ORDERLY LIFESTYLE

Read 2 Thessalonians 3:6–15.

What is the problem Paul deals with in this section of the letter?

Why did Paul not accept support from the church while in Thessalonica?

What were the "disorderly" doing?

How were the Thessalonians to deal with the disorderly?

In Lesson 9 the way we described Paul's directive to the Thessalonians was that everyone should mind his own business and have a business to mind (1 Thess. 4:11, 12). Paul's brief and gentle admonition in 1 Thessalonians was apparently unsuccessful, for he addresses the same issue again, and does so with considerably more force.

The force of Paul's exhortation is evident when one contrasts the terms he uses in 2 Thessalonians with his gentle directive in 1 Thessalonians. In 1 Thessalonians Paul said they should "aspire to lead a quiet life" (1 Thess. 4:11); this section of 2 Thessalonians begins with a command (2 Thess. 3:6). In 1 Thessalonians he told them to "mind your own business" (1 Thess. 4:11); in 2 Thessalonians he calls those who are not working "busybodies" (2 Thess. 3:11). Paul desires that they "walk properly" in 1 Thessalonians 4:12; whereas in 2 Thessalonians he reprimands the "disorderly" (2 Thess. 3:6, 11). The two words Paul uses, disorderly and busybody, show that Paul was being very direct—even blunt—in his correction.

   WORD WEALTH

Disorderly, *ataktos:* This word originally applied to soldiers marching out of order, or to a soldier who was not in his place or quit the ranks. Thus we see the picture of one who fails to conform to a prescribed rule, or (in 2 Thessalonians in particular) one who is idle or does not work.

Busybody, *peri-ergadzomai:* A combination of the prefix *peri,* around, and *ergadzomai,* to work; thus, to work around. The idea is that of a person who flits from task to task without really accomplishing anything. It is to busy oneself with trifling matters and to be inquisitive about the affairs of others.

The reason for the force of this correction is seen in the realization of two things. First, this was a repeated lesson that the church should have understood by then. Verse 10 makes one of the most direct statements of this principle, "If any will not work, neither shall he eat." Yet Paul says that is what they were taught when the apostles were with them. In addition to that teaching, the Thessalonians had been corrected in the first letter, and now the same lesson was needed in the second letter. Paul was getting tired of having to go over the same ground, so he deals with the issue at greater length and with more force.

But even more important to Paul than his frustration at the slow learning of the Thessalonians is the reason behind his teaching on this subject. Paul states his reason most clearly in 1 Thessalonians 4:12:

"That you may walk properly toward those who are outside, and that you may lack nothing." Paul was interested in three things here, two of which are obvious. He wished for the church to have a good reputation among the unbelievers, and the church also needed to have its own needs met. But a third aspect of this statement merges the two previous reasons. Part of their "lacking nothing" was for the benefit of those outside. If the church had its needs met, it could also be a source of charity and blessing to the outside world. Paul expresses this same idea in Ephesians 4:28:

> "Let him who stole steal no longer, but rather let him labor, working with his hands what is good, that he might have something to give him who has need."

Our lifestyle as Christians is to be directed toward others and orderly, yet these aspects are not the primary foci of our lives. Jesus said that the *first* command was to love the Lord your God (Matt. 22:37, 38). Our relationship with others is founded on our relationship with God, so we now consider what Paul has to say about our lives being God-directed.

A GOD-DIRECTED LIFESTYLE

Read 1 Thessalonians 5:16–28.
What is the overall tenor or attitude of this passage?

How does one pray without ceasing?

Comment on giving thanks in everything.

How does one quench the Spirit?

We are directed to "test all things." In context this would apply specifically to prophecies, but if prophecy is given by the Spirit, why do we need to test it?

Besides prophecy, what else does the command refer to?

How do we test all things?

This series of short commands is actually a treasure trove of material on our relationship with God. First, the order to rejoice must be viewed in proper light. If seen as a regulation, we can be left with the vision of the Marine sergeant standing over us yelling, "OK! We're gonna rejoice! Be happy—NOW!" That is obviously not the meaning of the apostle's words.

This opening statement should be seen as setting the tone for this whole passage. We are considering our relationship with God, and our relationship with God in Christ is no longer according to the Law. We need not come to God in fear because of our inadequacy; we can rejoice. Our relationship is joyful.

The concept of ceaseless prayer has always posed difficulties for people. It seems to be an impossibility. Most people say this means we should always be in an attitude of prayer. This is true, but I would like to suggest that we also look at that exhortation in light of the preceding and following verses.

These verses, taken together, give a pattern for prayer. First, prayer is begun with praise. Our rejoicing is based on who God is and on our relationship with Him in Christ. This realization brings forth praise as we come to God, our Father. Second, our prayers need to be continual in attitude, but they also need to be ceaseless in the sense that we are ready at any time to convert that attitude of prayer into active prayer. Third, ceaseless prayer is thankful. We give thanks to God for who He is and for what He does. In the midst of every situation we can thank God for at least one of those two things.

The next three verses apply to the work of the Spirit in the church. The Spirit is active in the Body of Christ, but He desires to be welcome as well. I don't know that the Spirit could be quenched to the point that He is totally absent from the church unless the church turn totally away from God. But we can hinder His work. The way not to hinder the work of the Spirit is to remember that the initial work of the Spirit in your life comes by "the hearing of faith" (Gal. 3:2). Having begun in the Spirit, it is only through faith, and not through the works of the flesh, that we continue to walk in the Spirit.

Paul also tells us not to despise prophecies. The character of the gift of prophecy spoken of in 1 Corinthians 12 and 14 is a much-debated topic today. Some believe that this gift referred primarily to the preaching of the Word, while others believe it was a divinely inspired utterance from the Spirit. Whatever your stand on that question, it is clear that the purpose of prophecy was for "edification and exhortation and comfort to men" (1 Cor. 14:3). The word itself also indicates this idea.

WORD WEALTH

Prophecies, *propheteia:* From *pro,* "forth," and *phemi,* "to speak." The primary use of the word is not predictive in the sense of foretelling, but interpretive, declaring or forth-telling, the will and counsel of God.[2]

The message we need to understand is not to despise the declaration of God's purpose however you believe it is done. However, we must judge without despising. Verse 21 applies directly to verse 20: we must test prophecies. Whether you believe the prophecy to be a spontaneous utterance or a prepared teaching, the command to test all things applies. The ground of truth is the Word of God, and that must form the basis of our testing of everything. Teaching which is in line with God's Word is good; hang on to it. But anything which fails to conform to the teaching of Scripture will eventually lead to evil.

Finally, Paul blesses the Thessalonians in the closing of his letter, and a particular aspect of his blessing is worthy of notice. Paul focuses on wholeness, unity of being. First, Paul's appeal is to the God of peace. The idea of peace includes the idea of wholeness or integration. When one is at peace, every part is united and working in harmony. Second, Paul asks that God sanctify them completely. Again Paul emphasizes the aspect of wholeness. And finally, Paul specifies every part of the person—spirit, soul and body. God's desire, spoken through Paul by the inspiration of the Spirit, is that His children continually grow towards wholeness.

FAITH ALIVE

The lifestyle we pursue is a lifestyle of wholeness. It is a lifestyle of wholeness in the sense that it requires all of our being and all of our relationships, and it is a lifestyle of wholeness in the sense that it produces wholeness.

As we close our study it is appropriate that we consider our relationships, for that is where our life is lived and our walk is walked. Begin by taking a few minutes to pray for your pastor or church leader; then consider the questions below.

Think of a fellow believer with whom you have difficulty getting along. How can the Lord teach you to minister to him or her with wisdom?

What can you learn from him or her?

What talents has God given you for the good of the Body? Are you using them?

God is working for our wholeness, yet He usually does that work through others. As we study and become more thoroughly grounded in the truth of the Word, let us continue also to grow in His grace as manifested in our relationship with God and our relationships with one another. "Now may the

Lord of peace Himself give you peace always in every way, The Lord be with you all." (2 Thess. 3:16).

1. *Spirit-Filled Life Bible* (Nashville, TN: Thomas Nelson Publishers, 1991), 1593, "Word Wealth: John 10:10, abundantly."

2. Ibid., 1831, "Word Wealth: 1 Thess. 5:20, prophecies."

Appendix I—
Introduction to Galatians

The basic questions which arise with reference to any books in the Bible are:

- Who wrote the book?
- When was the book written?
- To whom was the book written? and
- Why was the book written?

Secondary questions which arise usually can be related to one of these four questions.

In the case of Galatians, the big question is to whom was the book written? The question of when Galatians was written is closely connected to the question of audience, and there is broad consensus on the other two questions.

AUTHORSHIP AND PURPOSE

As stated above, there is virtually unanimous agreement that Paul wrote Galatians. There is no other book which has a stronger claim to Pauline authorship in both tradition and style.

The purpose of the letter is equally clear. Paul's opponents had gone into the territory where Paul had pioneered a work. They had taught new converts they had to be circumcised and keep the Law in addition to believing in Jesus Christ. The work of these Judaizers apparently met with some success, and their legalistic teaching was beginning to spread. Paul wrote Galatians as a zealous rebuke of those who had turned back to the Law, and to provide a solid, scriptural foundation for his teaching of justification by faith.

AUDIENCE

This is the big question in the criticism of Galatians, and there are two theories: the North Galatian theory and the South Galatian theory. The evidence around which the arguments turn is textual, grammatical, and historical. Some of the details get into grammatical distinctions in the original language, but we will look at some of the primary background and textual information.

The original Galatians were a Gaulish or Celtic people who migrated to central Asia Minor several hundred years before Christ. In the first century, the Roman province of Galatia included the original homeland of these people as well as a region further south which was home to people of Lycaonian or Phrygian descent. Late in the first century A.D. and early in the second century, the Roman emperors removed this southern portion from the province of Galatia, but in the time of Paul the cities he visited during his First Missionary Journey were in the southern part of the Roman province of Galatia.

The primary biblical evidence is found in Acts and Galatians. Luke records the visit to southern Galatia during the First Missionary Journey in Acts 13:13—14:28. In this passage he does not refer to Galatia, but speaks of Antioch in Pisidia (13:14) and refers to Lystra and Derbe as cities of Lycaonia (14:6). Luke does refer to Galatia twice: in Acts 16:6 and in Acts 18:23. In both those cases he speaks of the regions of Phrygia and Galatia together.

In Galatians 2:1–10, Paul speaks of a visit to Jerusalem. As explained in Lesson 1, there is disagreement on the identity of this visit, and that issue influences one's ideas about whom Paul addressed in Galatians. Also in Galatians, Paul speaks of his initial preaching of the gospel (4:13–15). The key issue in this passage is the statement in verse 13, ". . . I preached the gospel to you at the first." Some commentators feel this should be translated, ". . . I preached the gospel to you the former time." A "former time" would imply that Paul had made more than one visit to the Galatians when he wrote the letter.

With this background we can look at some of the main arguments for and against the two theories.

Proponents of the North Galatian view suggest that Paul and Luke use geographic or ethnic designations rather than official provincial names when referring to territories, thus Galatia refers to the northern part of the Roman province. However, opponents suggest that in writing to a group which included people from different ethnic groups, as well as Roman citizens, the only logical designation for Paul to use was the official provincial name.

A second argument concerns the visit to Jerusalem mentioned in Galatians 2. North Galatian proponents suggest it was the Jerusalem Council, which leaves open the question of why Paul did not mention the Council's decision when it so clearly dealt with the issues which the Galatians faced. South Galatian proponents suggested that it was the Famine Visit mentioned in Acts 11. This idea involves some chronological problems which we must examine more closely.

Jesus Christ was born between 6 and 4 B.C. He began His ministry when He was about thirty (Luke 3:23), which would be about A.D. 25 to 27. The length of His ministry cannot be determined precisely, but it could have been as short as two years or as long as three-and-a-half years. Therefore, the Crucifixion could have been as early as A.D. 27, and some put it as late as A.D. 33. Other evidence indicates that A.D. 30 or 33 are the best possibilities. This establishes the lower end of the time period into which we must fit the chronology of Paul's life as recorded in Acts and Galatians. The upper end of the time period involved would be the Jerusalem Council, which took place in A.D. 49.

In Galatians, Paul tells us of two visits to Jerusalem: one which was three years after his conversion, and a second which was fourteen years later. If the second visit is the Famine Visit, then the First Missionary Journey must also be included before the Jerusalem Council.

If the Crucifixion was in A.D. 33 and the times cited by Paul are consecutive, then obviously there is not enough time to fit the events of Paul's life into the time period available. Indeed, in that case we may have difficulties even if the Galatians 2 visit were the Jerusalem Council.

However, other possibilities must be considered. First, the three years and the fourteen years may overlap. Paul could be saying that he visited Jerusalem three years after his conversion and then again fourteen years after his conversion (eleven years after the first visit). This possibility, coupled with the possibility of the Crucifixion being in A.D. 30, provides adequate time for the events of Paul's life to fit in such a way that the Galatians 2 visit could be the Famine Visit. Here is a potential chronology:

Paul's conversion	A.D. 33
Post-conversion Visit	A.D. 36
Famine Visit	A.D. 47
First Missionary Journey	A.D. 47–48
Jerusalem Council	A.D. 49

Because of uncertainties regarding references and dates we cannot be absolutely sure which visit is referred to in Galatians 2. Neither view of the audience of Galatians can be ruled out solely on this basis.

A third point of discussion involves the visits to Galatia mentioned in Acts 16:6 and 18:23. The North Galatian proponents suggest that the churches to whom Galatians was written were established on the visit mentioned in Acts 16:6, and a second visit (mentioned in Acts 18:23) was made before the letter was written. They correlate this with the statement in Galatians 4:13 which may imply multiple visits.

South Galatian proponents bring out an additional argument from the text of Galatians regarding who is and is not mentioned in the letter. Barnabas figures prominently in the first two chapters of Galatians and is spoken of as one whom the Galatians know. Yet Acts tells us that Barnabas was Paul's companion only during the First Missionary Journey. If the North Galatian theory is true, then the churches to whom Paul was writing did not know Barnabas. North Galatian proponents point out that Galatians does not refer to Barnabas having been in Galatia, and the events involving Barnabas took place in Syria and Jerusalem—not Galatia. That being true, one still wonders why Paul would emphasize that "even Barnabas" (Gal. 2:13) was led astray if the Galatians did not know Barnabas.

In addition to the mention of Barnabas, one must explain the absence of any reference to Timothy. Timothy was working with Paul on the Second and Third Missionary Journeys when the Galatians were evangelized, according to the North Galatian theory. Additionally, Timothy is mentioned in all of Paul's letters except Ephesians, Titus, and Galatians. The lack of reference to Timothy can be logically explained by the assumption that Galatians was written before the Jerusalem Council, and thus before Timothy joined the apostolic band on the Second Missionary Journey. One argument made against this scenario is that Paul circumcised Timothy when Timothy joined him on the Second Missionary Journey (Acts 16:3). Yet in Galatians Paul writes, "Indeed I, Paul, say to you that if you become circumcised, Christ will profit you nothing" (Gal. 5:2).

Finally, the role of Peter in Galatians must be examined. Galatians 2 tells of Peter withdrawing from the Gentiles. This *could* have happened after the Jerusalem Council, but it is much easier to understand if it occurred before the Jerusalem Council.

There are a number of other details and issues which scholars debate with reference to these two theories, but the points we have covered provide a good overview of the issues involved. For further investigation of these issues, a good commentary on Galatians may be consulted. Thorough treatment of these issues, as well as others, is given by R. N. Longenecker in the *Word Biblical Commentary,* Volume 41, Galatians.

DATE

As explained in the preceding section, the date of the writing of Galatians depends heavily on the audience. If the North Galatian theory is true, then Paul probably wrote Galatians during his Third Missionary Journey. Most scholars who hold this view place the writing of Galatians at about A.D. 55 and believe that Paul probably wrote from Corinth at about the same time he was writing Romans.

On the other hand, the South Galatian view would place the writing before the Jerusalem Council, probably in A.D. 49. According to this view, Paul most likely wrote from Antioch in Syria prior to his attendance at the Council.

CONCLUSION

In spite of the North Galatian theory's longer history, I believe the overall evidence for the South Galatian theory is more persuasive. I believe that the splitting of the Roman province late in the first century and again in the second century led people to accept the northern area as the destination without questioning. After the traditional destination was fixed it remained unquestioned for a long time.

In addition, the historic record indicates that Paul generally spent some time in a location when he established a church. Acts 13 indicates that Paul was in Antioch of Pisidia for a number of weeks at the minimum. In Acts 14:3 Luke says the apostles were at Iconium "a long time." Acts 16:11 and 18 both indicate that a good deal of time was spent at Philippi when that church was established. Paul was worried about his work in Thessalonica because he had such a short time there, yet we know that he was in Thessalonica for three Sabbaths (Acts 17:2).

There is no record of Paul doing more than passing through the North Galatian region on his Second Missionary Journey, and he would have had time to do little else. We know that Paul established the church in Corinth in A.D. 50–51, so he probably arrived in Corinth in the fall of A.D. 50. The Jerusalem Council was in A.D. 49, and Paul returned to Antioch after the Council, so Paul could not have started on his Second Missionary Journey before summer of A.D. 49. Thus we have probably no more than fifteen months from the time Paul and Silas left Antioch until Paul was in Corinth. In this time period he visited the churches of South Galatia (Acts 16:1–6), and began churches in Philippi, Thessalonica, and Berea. We also know that he spent some time in Athens.

We can estimate that Paul spent two to three months in the areas where he established churches (except in Thessalonica, where he only spent about three weeks). In addition, he probably spent at least a few weeks at each of the four churches he had established on his First Missionary Journey. Add to that a few weeks spent in Athens, and we can account for about ten months out of a maximum of fifteen months, and these figures have not taken travel time into account. If we account for the time it took to travel over one thousand miles, mostly on foot, then we are reduced to probably only two months, at most, unaccounted for.

These facts coupled together indicate that Paul probably did not do extensive evangelization of the North Galatian area on his Second Missionary Journey. And if the North Galatian area was not evangelized until later, then there is another fact which tells against the North Galatian theory, and lends additional evidence to the South Galatian theory.

Appendix 2 — Introduction to Thessalonians

The letters to Thessalonica are significantly different than Galatians in both style and content. Thus, it is no surprise that there is more debate about the origins of these letters. In our brief study of the background of these letters we will focus on the same four questions which we addressed for Galatians:

- Who wrote the book,
- When was the book written,
- To whom was the book written, and
- Why was the book written?

AUTHORSHIP

Both letters to the Thessalonians traditionally have been attributed to Paul, yet the introduction itself lists Paul, Silvanus (Silas), and Timothy as the authors. In addition, the first person plural (we, us) is used throughout the letters. So there is no reason to doubt that Silas and Timothy had some input into the letters. But the fact that Paul is named first among the authors, along with the occasional first-person, direct reference to Paul (1 Thess. 2:18; 2 Thess. 3:17), indicates that Paul was the primary author.

Pauline authorship was not contested until the rise of modern criticism. Yet even with the rise of the more skeptical critics there is not much to be said against Pauline authorship.

Arguments have been made about the style and vocabulary not conforming to Paul's generally accepted works. This is easily rebutted in two ways: First, we really do not have enough of a body of writing by Paul to do an accurate analysis and second, the collaboration with Silas and Timothy could easily explain some variation in style, vocabulary, and content.

Some have taken the reference to wrath having come upon the Jews (1 Thess. 2:16) as a reference to the destruction of Jerusalem which occurred after Paul's death. However, there are other plausible events to which Paul could be referring, so that argument against Pauline authorship is weak.

Perhaps the biggest issue with reference to authorship relates to the relationship of the two letters to each other. There is a great deal of overlap, and also some very significant differences between the two letters. Some scholars have said that we would not have any problem with authorship if we had only one or the other of these two letters. But if each letter is acceptable on its own merits, one wonders why the existence of two similar letters should pose a problem. Nevertheless, some questions do arise which deserve attention.

The biggest question which arises pertaining to the relationship between 1 and 2 Thessalonians regards the teaching about the coming of Christ. It is said that the teachings of the two epistles are incompatible, for 1 Thessalonians teaches that the Second Coming will be sudden and unannounced; whereas 2 Thessalonians teaches that particular signs will precede the Second Coming.

The weight of this objection is overstated. A superficial reading may raise the question stated above, but more careful study shows that there is no conflict. In 2 Thessalonians Paul *does* indicate that signs will precede the Second Coming, but in 1 Thessalonians he indicates that it is unexpected only by the unbelievers (1 Thess. 5:1–4). Therefore, the teaching of the two letters is perfectly compatible.

Other questions and theories regarding the existence of two epistles are best treated under the questions of when and to whom Paul wrote these epistles, and it is to those questions we now turn.

DATE

The dating of the Thessalonian letters is very easy in one respect. The combination of internal and external evidence makes it clear that both letters were written around A.D. 50. The basic facts which fix this date are as follows:

- Paul was brought before the proconsul Gallio while in Corinth (Acts 18:12–17).
- We know from an inscription that Gallio was proconsul from A.D. 51–52.
- Paul was in Corinth for one-and-a-half years. We don't know when during this time that he was brought before Gallio, but most scholars believe it was toward the end of Paul's visit to Corinth.
- Therefore, Paul was probably in Corinth from the autumn of A.D. 50 to the spring of A.D. 52.
- Statements in 1 Thessalonians indicate that Paul was in Corinth when he wrote that letter (and 2 Thessalonians was written soon after).
- Thus, it was probably late in A.D. 50 or early in A.D. 51 when Paul wrote the Thessalonian letters.

An alternative possibility which has been considered is that 2 Thessalonians was written first. There is nothing inherently wrong with this theory—the order in the New Testament was assigned according to the length of the letter, not the chronology. According to this theory, Paul wrote 2 Thessalonians from Athens and sent it with Timothy when Timothy went to check up on the Thessalonians (1 Thess. 3:1, 2). Timothy brought back a good report, and Paul then wrote 1 Thessalonians.

This theory, though not inherently objectionable, raises more difficulties than it solves. The chief problems are that 1 Thessalonians 2:17—3:6 does not seem to make sense in a second letter, and 2 Thessalonians 2:2 and 15 refer to a previous epistle. Second Thessalonians 2:2 could refer to a theoretical possibility or to a forgery, but 2:15 seems definitely to refer to a previous letter.

AUDIENCE

The letters are addressed to the believers in Thessalonica, and we know that Paul established a church in that city which consisted of both Jewish and Gentile believers. The only issues raised by the question of audience relate to the relationship of the two letters to each other.

It has been suggested that the existence of the two letters can be explained by the presence of two groups of believers in Thessalonica—one Jewish and the other Gentile. This explains the similarities of the two letters: each group would have received a letter and many of the issues were common to both groups.

However, there is no record of there being two groups of believers, and it would have been very unlike Paul to allow such an aberration. Paul strongly supported the integration of all believers into one Body. For Paul to have allowed such a separation in Thessalonica is unthinkable.

It is more reasonable to believe that Paul wrote 1 Thessalonians to the whole (undivided) church of Thessalonica, and when the first letter did not adequately deal with all the problems which Paul wished to address, he wrote the second letter. This brings us to the question of why Paul wrote the letters. What were the issues which caused questions or problems to arise in the Thessalonian church?

PURPOSE

The purpose of the letters is most readily discerned from the letters themselves. The issues Paul was addressing in 1 Thessalonians fall into three broad categories: The apostles' conduct and encouragement, questions about the Second Coming, and the conduct of the Thessalonians.

The first half of 1 Thessalonians deals with the first issue. Paul writes a very warm and encouraging letter commending the Thessalonians for their steadfastness in the face of persecution. He also defended the conduct of the apostolic band, reminding the Thessalonians of how the apostles were examples. Apparently, opponents of Paul had been conducting a "smear campaign," and Paul found it necessary to remind the church that they worked for their own support and showed integrity at every point.

The issues of the conduct of the church and the end times are more closely related than it may seem. Questions directly relating to the Second Coming are dealt with, but there is also the question of how the believers should live in light of the imminence of the Lord's coming. It seemed that some believers were living off the church. They thought that the coming of the Lord was so near that they need do nothing but wait. Paul corrects this error and also gives direction concerning sexual conduct in the midst of their immoral society.

The second letter addresses many of the same issues. Obviously the first letter did not have the desired effect, and Paul was compelled to write again. The issue of the apostles' conduct was solved by the first letter, but more questions about the Second Coming had arisen and some believers still were being supported by the church when they should have been working. Paul devotes a large part of his second letter to discussing events of the end times. In addition, he gives a strong rebuke to the idle and provides definite direction for dealing with that problem.